From Surviving to Thriving

From Surviving to Thriving

Resources and Practical Strategies for New, Aspiring, and Veteran Superintendents

Rich Drolet
Armand Pires

THE SCHOOL SUPERINTENDENTS ASSOCIATION

ROWMAN & LITTLEFIELD
Lanham • Boulder • New York • London

Published by Rowman & Littlefield
An imprint of The Rowman & Littlefield Publishing Group, Inc.
4501 Forbes Boulevard, Suite 200, Lanham, Maryland 20706
www.rowman.com

86-90 Paul Street, London EC2A 4NE, United Kingdom

Copyright © 2023 by Rich Drolet and Armand Pires

All rights reserved. No part of this book may be reproduced in any form or by any electronic or mechanical means, including information storage and retrieval systems, without written permission from the publisher, except by a reviewer who may quote passages in a review.

British Library Cataloguing in Publication Information Available

Library of Congress Cataloging-in-Publication Data

Names: Drolet, Rich, 1976– author. | Pires, Armand, 1972– author.
Title: From surviving to thriving : resources and practical strategies for new, aspiring, and veteran superintendents / Rich Drolet, Armand Pires.
Description: Lanham, Maryland : Rowman & Littlefield, 2023. | Includes bibliographical references. | Summary: "This easy-to-read book provides actionable and practical strategies for any aspiring, new, or veteran school superintendent"—Provided by publisher.
Identifiers: LCCN 2023004109 (print) | LCCN 2023004110 (ebook) | ISBN 9781475868883 (cloth) | ISBN 9781475868890 (paperback) | ISBN 9781475868906 (epub)
Subjects: LCSH: School superintendents—United States—Handbooks, manuals, etc. | School management and organization—United States—Handbooks, manuals, etc. | School districts—United States—Administration—Handbooks, manuals, etc.
Classification: LCC LB2831.72 .D76 2023 (print) | LCC LB2831.72 (ebook) | DDC 371.2/011—dc23/eng/20230313
LC record available at https://lccn.loc.gov/2023004109
LC ebook record available at https://lccn.loc.gov/2023004110

Contents

Preface	vii
Acknowledgments	ix
Introduction	xi
Chapter 1: Welcome to the Superintendency: Your First Year: Congratulations, Condolences, Dos, and Don'ts	1
Chapter 2: Keep the Focus on Kids! It's All about Teaching and Learning	17
Chapter 3: Making New Friends: Nurturing Relationships with School Board Members	31
Chapter 4: Show Me the Money! Budget Development to Improve Student Learning	43
Chapter 5: Relationship Building: Being Out and About	55
Chapter 6: The Joys of Personnel Management: From Recruitment to Retirement	65
Chapter 7: Hear Ye, Hear Ye! Effective Communication Strategies	79
Chapter 8: I Need Help! Using Your Network	91
Chapter 9: The Sky Is Falling! Leading through Challenges and Crises	103
Chapter 10: Pulling It All Together	115
Notes	123
About the Authors	125

Preface

It was not too many years ago that we were new to the role of superintendent. Those early days, weeks, and months were full of self-doubt, questions, and a healthy dose of humility. While we had both been working in education and had served as educational leaders—including as teachers, assistant principals, principals, and assistant superintendents—there were many aspects of the school superintendent role that we did not understand.

In our early experience we struggled, made mistakes, and learned the hard way. Our training and experience had not prepared us to deal with the complex and highly nuanced role that we found ourselves in. The support of colleagues, patience of our school board chairs, and dedication of a team of educational leaders helped to foster our success in this role.

From Surviving to Thriving: Resources and Practical Strategies for New, Aspiring, and Veteran Superintendents will help aspiring, new, and veteran superintendents in new districts avoid the unseen pitfalls that can significantly impact or derail the new superintendent as they begin this work. Furthermore, the goal of this book is to help highlight crucial areas and behaviors that will support the success of the school superintendent and allow them to accelerate plans to improve the learning experience for students. Each chapter provides an overview of one key area of the role of school superintendent and how the reader can employ specific strategies to find success—to not only *survive*, but also *thrive*.

We hope that you find that this book supports you in your new role. We hope that you use it as another tool to find success in the incredibly important role of superintendent. We wish you well!

Acknowledgments

The idea for this book came about in a discussion during our earlier days as superintendents. We talked about the colleagues and allies who helped us through challenges, offered advice about how to move initiatives forward, and provided support when we needed someone to talk to. This book is dedicated to those committed superintendents, mentors, and colleagues who gave their time and expertise to ensure that we survived those early years. Without them, we would not have made it.

Introduction

From Surviving to Thriving: Resources and Practical Strategies for New, Aspiring, and Veteran Superintendents provides the educational leader with an easy-to-follow set of principles and strategies, organized by topic, to support any aspiring, new, or experienced superintendent to a new district as they strive for excellence.

This book includes ten chapters. The first nine chapters each cover an important facet of the role of the superintendent, while the last chapter pulls it all together, summarizing how these strategies will help you find success as a superintendent in your respective city or town.

The chapters in this book include information on the following topics.

CHAPTER 1: ENTRY PLANNING AND GOAL SETTING

As you begin your new role, entry planning and goal setting are important to gaining an understanding of your new district. Through the entry planning experience, you will identify strengths and opportunities that you will transparently communicate to the community. The identified opportunities will be merged and become part of your goals as you complete your entry plan. The first year will set the stage for improvement efforts in subsequent years.

CHAPTER 2: FOCUSING ON TEACHING AND LEARNING

The work of school superintendents must be centered on supporting and enhancing teaching and learning within the district. While many superintendents talk about "doing what is best for the kids" or "making decisions in the best interest of the students," shared strategies will provide you with concrete behaviors so that teaching and learning remain the main focus as superintendent. Strategies to help you stay close to what is happening in the classroom are shared and explored.

CHAPTER 3: NURTURING RELATIONSHIPS WITH SCHOOL BOARD MEMBERS AND OTHER OFFICIALS

The school board has an important role to play in ensuring that students' needs are met. Your responsibility as superintendent is to provide support and direction to the school board so that there is an alignment of goals and focus areas. Critical to that alignment—and success—is the highly collaborative and productive relationships forged among the superintendent and school board members.

This chapter offers strategies to create opportunities for relationship building and partnering to avoid unnecessary distractions with the goal of meeting the needs of students. In addition, the important relationships between the superintendent and other elected and appointed officials within the community are explored. Lastly, relationship building with other elected and appointed officials within your community is discussed.

CHAPTER 4: LEVERAGING THE BUDGET DEVELOPMENT PROCESS FOR IMPROVEMENT

The budget of any school or district can be many millions of dollars. Most superintendents traditionally have little to no experience in finance. This knowledge gap can result in missed opportunities for improving the student experience. This chapter shares ways to improve your knowledge base around district finance, forge a productive relationship with your school district's chief financial officer, and utilize effective budgeting practices.

Other areas covered in this chapter include advocating for school capital improvements, setting a yearly budget calendar while soliciting school board input regarding what type of budget to build, setting goals throughout the budget process, using data to advocate for new positions or programs, placing input from stakeholders into the budget development process, and communicating transparently with other town or city boards.

CHAPTER 5: RELATIONSHIP BUILDING AND BEING VISIBLE

The position of superintendent can be one that intimidates others. An important goal is for you to be approachable and actively engaged in your community. Superintendents need to make efforts to develop positive relationships with all constituents. They must communicate with individuals or entire groups outside of the schools, or with community members with children in the district. It is vital for the public to view the superintendent of schools as a positive leader of the most important organization in the town or city, one who is deeply invested in the community.

CHAPTER 6: GETTING THE BEST OUT OF YOUR PEOPLE

School districts have hundreds or thousands of individuals who show up at schools to make the very best experience for students. As superintendent, you are ultimately responsible for all aspects of the employee experience. This often is another area where a new superintendent may not have a great deal of experience. The complexities of multiple employee groups, likely with collectively bargained agreements, further complicates this work.

This chapter focuses on providing the superintendent with proactive strategies to engage in recruiting, hiring, and onboarding employees. Additionally, it covers strategies that the school superintendent can use to ensure that the district is a great place to work in order to foster staff longevity and a positive work culture. Finally, difficulties within human resources are outlined and shared.

CHAPTER 7: COMMUNICATION STRATEGIES TO SUPPORT ENGAGEMENT AND TRANSPARENCY

One of the most frequent complaints a superintendent will hear is related to communication—for example, someone did not know something but feel like they should have known. This chapter outlines approaches to support a robust and transparent communication strategy. This includes in-person meetings, email, and social media avenues. Discussion of developing communication plans is a key element of this chapter, with an example of what that should look like.

CHAPTER 8: IDENTIFYING SUPPORTS FOR YOURSELF

The role of the superintendent is demanding, emotionally exhausting, and the most fulfilling work that most of us will ever engage in. To ensure that a superintendent has the stamina to continue the work, it is important that they regularly connect with, and gain support from, colleagues and professional organizations. This is a critical determinant of success; superintendents should avoid going at it alone, and instead rely on their peers for camaraderie, encouragement, and support.

CHAPTER 9: MANAGING CHALLENGES AND CRISES

As superintendent, there will almost always be a daily crisis or potential crisis that you will have to address. There are successful approaches you can take to prevent crises or manage them when they occur. Understanding what type of crisis is occurring is key to developing a response strategy. This chapter will share some keystone behaviors to support success while leading through a crisis.

CHAPTER 10: PULLING IT ALL TOGETHER

Topics in this book are ones that have been identified to be among the greatest pitfalls—when not handled well—for a new superintendent. Taking the time to better understand the challenges within each of these areas will enhance a school superintendent's overall skills and provide support for success. Ultimately, the more effectively a superintendent manages these complex topics, the more likely they will be able to engage in meaningful and sustained improvement to better the learning experience for their students. This is, after all, the ultimate "why" for us.

Chapter 1

Welcome to the Superintendency

Your First Year: Congratulations, Condolences, Dos, and Don'ts

EXPERIENCES FROM THE FIELD

When I was offered the school superintendent job and signed my first contract as a new superintendent, I was elated; however, I didn't know where to begin. Without knowing anyone in my new school district, and the outgoing superintendent unavailable, I was somewhat rudderless.

I knew I wanted to get to know as many teachers, administrators, parents, students, staff, board members, and community members as possible. But I wasn't sure where to start, who to trust, and what initiatives to prioritize. Once I learned some key strategies from other experienced school superintendents, I was more proactive than reactive, and things flowed better as the school year progressed.

Once I learned some must-do strategies for new superintendents, I was able to communicate my core values. Next I formulated a superintendent entry plan. Then I gathered feedback from constituents to formulate some district goals, and then develop a sensible budget for the subsequent school year. As a result, year two as the superintendent allowed me to advocate for more resources for students in an informed way, provide some long-term direction, and work collaboratively with the entire school community.

BEGINNING HIGHS AND NEW CHALLENGES AHEAD

Congratulations! Becoming a school superintendent has taken many years of education, hard work, and perseverance. You have demonstrated great skills in your service as an educational leader, problem solver, and effective communicator. You should be proud of yourself for moving up the ranks and earning this prestigious position. Take this moment to enjoy this achievement—now it is time to get to work.

You may or may not be aware of the many challenges that lie ahead. There is a benefit to not knowing what awaits you as a school superintendent, as the work can be extraordinarily challenging and overwhelming. Every superintendent has to react at times, and in the moment, to various situations that may arise.

New superintendents also need to be proactive to strategically meet the challenges that coincide with any new superintendent position—yet this is often difficult when an overwhelming number of urgent matters require your attention. This chapter addresses the highs and the lows, the dos and the don'ts, and provides a game plan new superintendents can implement to make their first year as superintendent as successful and productive as possible.

The Honeymoon Period

Remember when you got the email or call informing you of your selection by the new superintendent screening committee for an interview? And then the next call you received shared the exciting news that you made it through the first round of interviews? Then you were selected as a finalist!

Perhaps you also remember other, more disappointing calls or notifications, when you received the message that you were not selected for an interview, or were told after your first or second interview that you would not be moving forward to the next round. Maybe you did not have to go through a thorough vetting process, and instead you were promoted from within to the new superintendent opening, rising or being promoted from your assistant superintendent or principal position.

How about the excitement of that last call when you were told you were selected for the superintendent position and would be sent a draft superintendent contract for review or to negotiate? Seems like ages ago, doesn't it? Regardless of which process you experienced in becoming a school superintendent, you persevered through the process.

Those were memorable times. Everyone you met seemed so excited about your arrival to your new superintendent seat. Many people offered important advice on how to do better than your predecessor, or shared their impression of what the district really needed. In those early days, everything was going well. That first summer you felt good, and you really seemed to gel with these new people who chose you, and truly seemed to like you.

Reality Can Bite

People met you and shook your hand, looked you up and down, and said, "Congratulations!" and "We are so excited that you are here!" But you can bet that some of them were really thinking, "I wonder how long you will last." Or maybe they were thinking, "I feel bad for you!" Some of these people may have respectfully shared their concerns to you as the new superintendent, or they told you some of the historical context related to certain aspects of the school district.

And then you started to meet some *other* people, who perhaps were not as excited about your arrival. Maybe they openly stated their allegiance to your predecessor, or they warned you of all the weaknesses in the school system. Some may have been trying to offer sage advice by telling you what to prioritize before you even had a chance to conduct your first "get to know you" sit-downs with key individuals in your new district or new role.

THE SUPERINTENDENT POSITION IS DIFFERENT BUT SIMILAR

It's Different from Other Jobs You've Had in Education . . .

Let's face it—the superintendent job is quite different from other jobs you have had in education. In those other positions you have likely excelled, which is how you got to this point. In this new position, you are not confined to managing one building, or filling one specific role such as curriculum or finances.

You have an overwhelming number of areas of responsibility—in fact, *everything* about the district is now your responsibility. Unlike your previous experience, you have built skills and knowledge over time that have helped you along the way. In your new role as superintendent of schools, there are many unknowns.

You don't present your individual school budget to your teachers, or a parent-teacher organization, or a school council governing group, for example. You need to present your budget to everyone. This includes faculty and staff in the district, the school board, select board or town council, and the finance committee. You might even find yourself presenting the budget at the local senior center.

Maybe you had your own administrative assistant as a principal or assistant superintendent, but now you have a designated administrative assistant. This person should not only help you with your job tasks and letter writing, but also help you to manage your daily and weekly calendar, set and keep appointments with various constituents, and talk to parents who call or email about an issue. Ideally, an administrative assistant will also try to help you maintain a healthy work/life balance.

. . . But There Are Some Similarities to the School Principal Position

Although the superintendent job is undoubtedly more complex than previous jobs you have held in education, there are many parallel and transferable skills between your previous positions and your new responsibilities as superintendent. For example, the skills you displayed when working with the parent-teacher organization or school council will support your successful interaction with the school board. Your excellent communication skills, which you leveraged to ensure that constituent groups were clear on your mission and vision for a school or program, are acted out on a larger scale with a more diverse stakeholder group.

The superintendent role is also lonely like many other jobs in school administration. Hopefully you are comfortable with that reality. You have some trusted people in your circle with whom you can confide about the difficulties related to the school superintendent job, occasionally unwind, and seek out for advice.

It's More Complex Than Other Jobs You've Had in Education . . .

The superintendent job is more political, more social, more personal, and more visible than other positions you have held in education. In addition to the internal players within the school district, you now have to deal with many other constituent groups within the city or town. In some cases you are asked to answer questions, or weigh in on planning that includes topics for which you have had little to no experience.

The role includes an ever-changing body of work: Celebrating staff and student successes district-wide. Public records requests. Hiring principals and administrators. Press releases to manage public relation issues. Dealing with local newspapers, television shows, and resident taxpayers who do not have children in the schools.

Don't forget district strategic plans. Personnel issues. Long-term suspensions and expulsions. School safety threats. Student and staff injuries. Collective bargaining. Managing a wide variety of crises. And the list goes on and on.

... But It Can Be Simpler in Some Ways, Too

A significant amount of your time should be spent doing relatively simple things that keep you visible and connected within your community. Plan to spend time attending events, celebrating student accomplishments, mingling, and socializing. Make sure you socialize in a professional manner—do not gossip, keep personnel matters confidential, and try to represent your school district with dignity and respect.

If you are a social being and do not mind gathering and chatting informally, this will come easily for you. If you struggle because you are an introvert, or have anxiety in social settings (sometimes we all do), work at it. Do not always socialize with the same people at events, as this may lead observers to think you play favorites.

Oversee and manage the work. Do not get overly involved in minutiae or details unless something requires you to do so. You should have layers of directors or other subordinates to whom you can delegate certain items. Much of your time should be spent making phone calls, meeting with constituents, and serving as a coach or advisor to principals and other staff. Act like a baseball manager setting the lineups—make the key substitutions, and direct what pitches should be thrown.

DOS AND DON'TS WHEN STARTING YOUR NEW SUPERINTENDENCY

Do Spend Considerable Time in Your New District as Soon as You Can

You should be excited about your new superintendency, so you need to be sure to act on that feeling. Ask to visit the school district and begin to attend some social events in your new district before your actual start date (unless you are asked not to visit before your official start date out of respect for the transition of an outgoing superintendent). If you are promoted from within, and the scenery is not so new, start doing some things in the new role.

You might spend some of the transition time shadowing the outgoing superintendent before they leave, learning about the budget process, or meeting with new constituents. If you need to distance yourself from the outgoing superintendent, find useful ways to support your transition that will give you a jump start when you officially transition.

Don't Overextend Yourself or Let the Job Define Who You Are

When we meet and connect with other superintendents at conferences or workshops or through networking events, it is not just because we are all superintendents (although that is how we have come together at events). It is because we want that personal connection. We may find that we have certain things in common as we talk about our families; we may discover that we share an affinity for a particular type of music or sports team; we may bond over conversing about people we mutually know or have worked with.

You are now a superintendent of schools, but you could have been an accountant, social worker, engineer, stay-at-home parent, or remained a teacher until retirement. It is important to spend quality time outside of the superintendent job, reading or gardening, playing sports or exercising, hanging out with friends, going to the beach or the mountains, or just relaxing at home. While this may seem trivial here, it will become an important therapy as the work becomes more stressful and cumbersome.

Do Make the Tough Decisions When Needed

Decision making is an important aspect of the job. Making hard decisions is not for the faint of heart and can result in challenging circumstances. Although some people may be disappointed or resentful about some of your decisions, or may hold this against you in the future, you were hired to make decisions—including the difficult ones—to benefit students.

When preparing to make a difficult decision, it is helpful to keep a few things in mind:

- Make sure your decision aligns with the district's core values and is in the best interest of students.
- Provide a clear rationale for the decision that you have made.
- When engaged in conversations with those who do not agree, be sure to engage empathetically and listen carefully to those areas of concern.

Making difficult decisions can be challenging. Without realizing it, some school superintendents often engage in "delay tactics" because they may need time for additional analysis of a particular topic. Superintendents often need to mull things over, communicate with others before making a decision, and consider multiple perspectives.

This behavior for a school superintendent is normal, but eventually a decision needs to be made. Taking too much time before making an ultimate decision can lead to "analysis paralysis" and result in an approach that is too tentative. A school superintendent's credibility can be eroded over the long run if they are unwilling to make tough decisions.

When making decisions, focus on the key issues, and think about what is in the best interest of the students or the school district. Get to the heart of the matter, consult others as needed, and do what you think is the right thing. Then make the best decision that you can. It is that simple.

And when making decisions, be careful not to play favorites, or not to let others *think* you may be playing favorites. Expediency and competency are needed, but unless speed is required, school superintendents can usually take some time to consider multiple perspectives first, then make their decision after all the facts have been gathered and options have been weighed.

Don't Forget to Think about How Your Decisions May Be Received, Perceived, and Grieved

Just as critical as making decisions is thinking about how those decisions may impact others. First and foremost, think about how each decision will impact students. If it will help students, aligns to the core values of the school district, and moves the needle on school or district improvement forward, it is likely the right thing to do.

You also need to consider how your decisions will affect relationships between the town and the schools. For example, bargaining a new teacher contract is an example for which you might need to at least connect with the mayor or town administrator before coming to a final collective bargaining agreement.

Preferably, you should have these discussions prior to bargaining so that you know what your bottom line is (i.e., highest amount you can give the teachers in the next contract). School boards should be part of negotiations unless they have given you complete autonomy to handle the collective bargaining.

In thinking about making exceptions or overriding contract language for certain staff (particularly exceptions to a collective bargaining agreement), school superintendents need to be fair and consistent. Union grievances may be expected, and should be viewed as a dispute resolution process. When a grievance reaches your desk, make sure that you give the school board chairperson a heads-up on the issues.

Your principals should do the same with you when a teacher grieves one of their decisions. This communication process will help especially if you deny the grievance; that way your school board will have already heard your sound rationale and be more prone to support your denial.

Do Use Your Position as a Means to Improve the Lives of Your Students

On a positive note, you now have more authority and influence to improve the experience for students when you wield the superintendent wand. Think about how you can use that influence and authority to do good things. Specifically, we are talking about doing good things for the students for whom you are responsible. For example, work with the high school principal to adjust the high school schedule to create more time for instruction or for adding additional learning pathways, internships, or career opportunities for secondary students to explore.

Serve as a positive role model to in-district colleagues by actively advocating for students, in particular those most in need. Examine existing practices to determine whether practices in your district are fair and equitable for all students. For example, review homework policies and practices, secondary grading practices, teacher assignment practices, and how students are placed into honors or Advanced Placement courses, or other special programs.

Lead district leadership team walkthroughs to gather data on where instructional improvements might need to be made. Coach your principals to have high expectations, hold staff accountable, and make decisions in the best interest of all kids.

Don't Use Your Position to Gain Favors or Perks

Being a superintendent is a privilege you have earned, not your given right. We have all seen stories of colleagues who, once in the role, have stepped over the line. As a highly visible public servant, it is critically important that you behave in ways that are ethical and beyond reproach, and in a manner that provides modeling for those around you.

People are watching you. Model what you expect of all district employees. Do not accept gifts or special favors. Use your own personal money if you buy staff gifts, and pay to attend other social events as needed.

We've all read stories or seen on the news about a superintendent who used their influence or power for personal gain. Don't do that. Doing shady things brings shame and ridicule to the profession. It can also end your superintendency or bring your career to a screeching halt.

YOUR FIRST SIX TO NINE MONTHS

Participate in a New Superintendent Program

New superintendents undoubtedly will benefit from participating in a new superintendent program. In opening negotiations with school boards, new superintendents should ascertain that this invaluable professional development is funded as part of their new superintendent contract or district professional development funds. It is important that a new superintendent knows about the programs that might be available through their state organization or AASA, The School Superintendents Association.

Participation may be in person or virtual. It is most important that a new superintendent identifies supportive induction programs as they start their new position. A new superintendent induction program should focus on providing you with strategies as you enter the position to lay the groundwork to accelerate student learning.

For example, in Massachusetts, nearly all new superintendents have participated in the New Superintendent Induction Program (NSIP).[1] This program is sponsored by both the Massachusetts Association of School Superintendents (M.A.S.S.) and the Massachusetts Department of Elementary and Secondary Education (DESE). The NSIP's goal is to empower new superintendents to accelerate student learning through strategic leadership.

As part of Massachusetts' three-year-long NSIP, new superintendents are allowed to engage in intensive full-day sessions: eight days in year 1, five days in year 2, and then continued one-on-one coaching sessions and small group regional cohort sessions in year 3. The in-person days are mostly led by retired school superintendents who have deep experience as superintendents in the state.

Practicing superintendents also sometimes participate to present on particular topics, impart advice, and note lessons learned through living through and overcoming challenges experienced on the job. Another critical aspect of NSIP is that each new superintendent is paired with a superintendent coach they can get feedback from after a visit to their school district, and talk to or meet with for about six hours a month.

Establish an Entry Plan

The development of an entry plan is an essential early step in your superintendency. You should consider developing your entry plan prior to beginning your new position. A formal plan will help you engage in an articulate process of gathering information and assessing your new district's history, personnel, policies, and procedures prior to making any planned changes.

An entry plan will ensure, and let others know, that critical time and attention will be focused on gaining a broad perspective from stakeholders within and outside of the school system. This plan will assist you in remaining focused on gathering information about the community and the organization, establishing a strong school and community presence, identifying critical issues, building on strengths, and creating a network of contacts to assist you in the work of improving the schools.

A thorough entry plan will include phases and should take about nine to twelve months to complete. The first phase is when you listen and learn, visit classrooms, go to school and community events, host parent coffee hours, interview constituents, read school district literature, and provide the school board with updates along the way.

The second phase is the time to analyze and engage, review school district data, task your district leadership team to review strengths, identify areas in need of improvement, and look for opportunities present in the district.

The last phase is when you lead and strategize, use the information you have gathered, share what you have learned in a transparent manner, identify new district goals, and publish the next steps.

The individual interviews with various constituents should give you a mountain of information to consider. Most people will want to share what they know about the history of the school district. It is likely that many individuals and groups will engage with you honestly about the strengths and challenges of the district during these interviews. New school superintendents should use people's earnest and honest feedback from these interviews to move the school district forward.

Write and Publish Your Report of Entry Findings

After about six to nine months into your new school superintendent job, you need to share what you've learned about the school district with the community. Your report of entry findings is the result of your completed entry plan. It should summarize what you have seen, heard, and counted in your first months in your new superintendency.

Ideally, a report of entry findings will outline the next steps that will be critical for the development of future district goals, strategic objectives, and action steps. This will enable your school district to focus on continuous growth and improvement.

In the report of entry findings, you want to highlight the process that you used to immerse yourself in the daily life of the schools. Results should include specific information and collected data related to school and principal visits, meetings with a wide array of constituents, and information about the school district. You would then write about or communicate how you analyzed this information to identify strengths, areas in need of improvement, and opportunities or untapped potential.

You want others to know *how* you arrived at your findings, summarizing what you have counted, heard, and seen in this report. Take care in preparing this report because it will be used broadly as the rationale for the decisions you are making, and the leadership behaviors you are engaging in, relative to strategic activities.

Examples of the data (counted) that you may incorporate in your report include the following:

- Student achievement data (both state and local)
- Enrollment data and projections
- Special education data
- Fiscal audits and information

Some examples of what you have heard would have come from constituent interviews, parent coffee hours, chatting with students and staff, or listening to school board feedback. Lastly, examples of what you have seen would be school and classroom visits, interactions among staff and community members, and how various other city or town meetings have transpired.

In your entry report, you should highlight major findings and impressions, of course being sure to mention all of the positive things happening in the district, as well as identifying areas the school district should address. Include essential questions to further explore each major finding, which should aim to guide you and the school district in your future work.

Findings could be related to community support, student learning, staffing, professional development, special education programming, or other budget priorities. Toward the end of the report, be sure to mention next steps, which should help to drive discussion, inquiry, healthy debate, and motivation to set up future action plans to continue to improve the school district.

Communicate Your Core Values

In addition to helping the community get to personally know you better, community members want to know what you stand for and what you *value*. You likely discussed this—a lot—during the interview process. In case you have not yet articulated your core values in a succinct and clear way, now is the time.

Do not feel like you have to do this work yourself. Find someone who will push you to further contemplate your core values. Use the resources around you, such as your coach from the new superintendent program, a consultant who can spend a few hours facilitating this discussion, or a retired superintendent whom you feel did this well.

Your core values, once refined, should become part of nearly all of your communications, in part or in whole. Consider how you will pepper statements about your core values throughout nearly all of your communications, conversations, and interactions. This redundancy will reinforce the belief system that guides your work and will continue to communicate to the community how initiatives and articles are connected to your core values.

All of your behaviors, and the decisions you make, should be informed and influenced by your core values. To create core values, start by writing down what is most important to you educationally and professionally. Next, categorize them as themes into three to five identifiable and relatable areas. And finally, refine them. Think of examples you could share that reinforce how your core values relate to education within your school district. See table 1.1, which outlines four core values created, written, and communicated by one of the superintendent authors.

Table 1.1 Sample Cores Values and Explanation of Core Values

Core Value	Explanation of the Core Value
Centrality of the Classroom	There is nothing more important than the work happening in the classroom between the teacher and the student. The teacher–student relationship is sacred. Teaching and learning are what is most important. We want to celebrate and support great teaching.
Respect and Respecting Differences	We firmly believe in equality and providing students with experiences that teach them to be accepting of differences and to show respect to others. Some of the most influential figures who have left an impact on me are Mahatma Gandhi and Martin Luther King Jr.
Collegiality	There is a big difference between collegiality and congeniality. Congeniality is being cordial and nice to one another; collegiality requires more effort—it is learning together, acting professionally in a work environment, cooperating and compromising, and coming together in our schools to provide equitable, authentic, relevant, enriching, and meaningful learning experiences for our students.
Good Communication	Like respecting differences, the need for good communication is obvious. It involves working hard to return emails and phone calls within twenty-four hours, sharing in the successes of others, showing gratitude, listening well, and providing direct and constructive feedback for learning and future improvement. It also involves being transparent and proactive in explaining rationale for decisions when appropriate—decisions that should be grounded in what is the best interest of the students.

Share Your Superintendent Goals

Given the typical cadence of when new superintendents begin their positions, you will likely start in your new role when the district is in summer recess. During that first summer, you will be actively engaged in implementing your entry plan. Shortly after starting you will need to begin contemplating your goals for your first year. Once your entry plan work has begun and you have shared your core values with the community, it is time to draft your annual superintendent goals.

When doing so, keep your superintendent goals simple and think about some long-term goals that you may be able to extend into future years. Typically, superintendents will need to submit goals for their school board to approve no later than the fall of the school year. Entry and direction setting could be your district goal, since implementing your entry plan and then sharing your report of entry findings will take most of your first year. Your professional goal could be to participate in a new superintendent induction program, work with a mentor, or participate in some other professional development that will assist in your transition to the superintendent role.

WRAPPING UP YOUR FIRST YEAR

Reflect on Progress You Made Toward Your Beginning-of-Year Superintendent Goals

Your superintendent goals should have included some quarterly or semi-annual benchmarks to try to meet throughout your first year. But even if you did not have the opportunity to reflect on your goals during your hectic first year, you can reflect on them in the spring of year 1 and share the progress you have made working toward your goals with the school board.

Some goals may have been accomplished. Some goals may need to be continued into year 2 (this happened a lot during the COVID-19 pandemic as superintendents' typical work was significantly disrupted for two years). Some school superintendent goals may even need to be scrapped altogether if the trajectory of the superintendent's work in your district changed significantly based on what you learned that you needed to reprioritize in year 1.

Use Your State's Superintendent Evaluation Process

Even if the school board or previous superintendent historically has not participated in a formalized superintendent evaluation process, it is important for you as a new superintendent to use the superintendent evaluation process.

This lets the board know you are interested in cross-referencing the work you have done against the state's expectations for the superintendent.

Reading and reflecting on the indicators for each superintendent standard allows you to see where you may need to spend more time to improve. Reflecting on your state's superintendent standards might help you to realize that you could do more to improve school safety or to make the school experience more inclusive or equitable for certain subgroups of students, for example.

Use the school board superintendent evaluation process to show your board how you have done comprehensive work in your first year. One suggested practice is to link particular artifacts to document how you have met specific standards you are tasked to meet as part of the superintendent job. Justify the work you have done by linking your reflections to your state superintendent standards and indicators. This will demonstrate that you are proficient or exemplary in certain areas of the work from your first year.

Also, we recommend that you provide this evidence to your school board a few weeks in advance of their public evaluation of you. It is possible that superintendents before you may not have had to do this. This practice of utilizing the formalized superintendent evaluation process should impress upon your school board how you are a reflective practitioner, and that you are willing to adjust the important work that you do based on the ever-evolving needs of the students in your school district.

Consider a 360-Degree Feedback Approach

As discussed early in this chapter, the role of superintendent can be very lonely. As reflective practitioners and successful educational leaders, we should always be open to receiving feedback. This role is unique in that you may find it is difficult to receive honest feedback about your performance, especially as you complete your first year.

Let there be no doubt that throughout your first year you will receive lots of feedback. This will come in welcome and unwelcome ways, from known and unknown sources. Will you be able to integrate that feedback into your deeper reflection on your successes and opportunities in your first year?

As a new superintendent, you are also modeling leadership behaviors for other members of your leadership team. Implementing a 360-degree feedback model will allow you to gain valuable insight into your practice. Through an anonymous feedback tool, you will solicit feedback from colleagues about your effectiveness as superintendent.

Using this approach, you may find a higher threshold of receptivity for the feedback you are given. Since it will come from colleagues that you have identified, you can rely on the source. This approach will allow you to be more open and reflective of your practices in the first year—both your successes and opportunities.

There are many excellent examples of anonymous feedback forms that you can use. The areas of focus are up to you, but the feedback should be connected to the goals that are established for your first year.

CONCLUSION

By the end of your first year as a superintendent, there are many new people with whom you likely have developed great relationships. Some of these relationships may have been formed easily; others might have required more work. Use this time at the end of your first year to reflect on *how* you can improve relationships, and with *whom* you should improve relationships or conduct further outreach.

Superintendents should think about some constituents with whom they may need to build stronger relationships or more trust. These individuals could be union members, other city or town leaders, groups of students, parent groups, certain teachers or administrators, or even individual school board members. Improving individual relationships should always be the heart of the work.

Breathe

Now that you have completed your first school year, and learned some dos and don'ts, take some time to breathe, unwind, and reach out to those people who supported you along the way. Celebrate the accomplishment of completing your first year by making some summer vacation plans with your family and loved ones. Rejuvenate and prepare for year 2. After all, there will be plenty of time to work on strategic plans and begin doing the work to improve the experience for students.

EXPERIENCES FROM THE FIELD

Being a new superintendent in a school district brings many opportunities and challenges. Taking advantage of the opportunities is tantamount to success. Getting to know new people, communicating your core values, setting direction, working with a coach or other new superintendents, sharing what you learn with others, and then advocating for resources will boost your credibility and let constituents know you are a competent, caring, and dedicated new superintendent.

ADDITIONAL RESOURCES

Cheatham, J., R. Thomas, and A. Parrott-Scheffer. *Entry Planning for Equity-Focused Leaders: Empowering Schools and Communities*. Cambridge, MA: Harvard Education Press, 2022.

Huetteman, L. *The Value of Core Values: Five Keys to Success through Value-Centered Leadership*. Trenton, GA: Booklocker.com, 2012.

"The Massachusetts Model System for Educator Evaluation: Evaluating Superintendent and District-Level Administrators." Massachusetts Department of Elementary and Secondary Education. Accessed January 1, 2023. https://www.doe.mass.edu/edeval/model/evaluating-superintendents.pdf.

"Newly Appointed Superintendents Academy." American Association of School Administrators. Accessed January 1, 2023. https://www.aasa.org/newly-appointed.aspx.

Chapter 2

Keep the Focus on Kids!
It's All about Teaching and Learning

EXPERIENCES FROM THE FIELD

In my first few months as a new superintendent the majority of my time was spent working on a new building project, tending to school board requests, and managing personnel issues. In retrospect, although these things were important, I was not entirely doing what I should have.

Teaching and learning should have been my main focus. When I finally started to prioritize teaching and learning initiatives, we gained momentum for principals and staff to start to improve many learning experiences for our students. I realized how vital it was to spend more time working toward what is most sacred—trying to improve classroom learning experiences as well as outcomes for our students. If I could go back, I would have started straight out of the gate with a more clear and articulated focus on teaching and learning.

KEEPING PRIORITIES STRAIGHT

Just like school principals, superintendents can easily occupy their days, weeks, and months keeping busy with administrative tasks, communications, evaluations, or simply even reacting to whatever happens each day by managing crises. But what makes a school principal an effective educational leader? It is those principal leaders who keep a laser-like focus on improving teaching and learning, while also working to create conditions for people to do their best work, who take the prize.

Too often, superintendents can become victims to the job. At times the superintendency will force you to act on urgent issues of lower importance while largely ignoring teaching and learning. But superintendents need to remember that, with the exception of student and staff safety, *there is nothing more important than teaching and learning.*

Focused and sustained instructional improvements are the heart of the work of a school superintendent. Superintendents should try to focus on one or two initiatives at a time related to making improvements to instructional practices and learner outcomes. A superintendent who juggles too many goals or initiatives at once may ultimately drop the ball, or drown in their own ambition. Focusing and then following through on the successful implementation of one or two educational initiatives at a time may prove to be the most beneficial, and certainly more doable, path for a school superintendent.

Remember Your Roots

Too often superintendents who started off as teachers stray from their roots. Even though superintendents are now more removed from the classroom in their roles, they should still think as the best educators do. The best educators are always trying new things, working to get the lightbulb to turn on for their learners, and striving to improve their instructional practices. Superintendents should continue to do the same, always thinking about how they can make things better for the students and staff in their school districts.

Most educators did not start off their careers in education in order to become school superintendents. First and foremost, individuals who chose education did so because of the mission and joy of learning, helping others, and working with kids. Think of the first school building you worked in. What a privilege it was to get our first job in education working with students entrusted to us by their families.

Unless you are done with learning, sick of helping others, and tired of working with kids, the superintendency should also be thought of as a privilege, not a burden. Even though school superintendents admittedly have to work more directly with adults than with students now, and oftentimes working with adults may not be as much fun as working with kids, superintendents need to continue to do what they did as new teachers or educators: enjoy learning, help others, and work with students.

THE BRUNT OF THE WORK GETS DONE THROUGH OTHERS

Although being a school superintendent brings new pressures, stressors, and leadership challenges, it is important to keep in mind that the brunt of the work gets done by people *other* than the superintendent. Teachers write the lesson plans, grade the papers, and manage the majority of students and parents. Principals also deal with many students and families, as well as deal with their staff and school facilities. Assistant superintendents help to define instructional goals, align curriculum to state standards, and write grants. And school business managers ensure that the fiscal house is in order and the district is in sound fiscal health.

District superintendents oversee and lead many projects, initiatives, and people, but they usually don't *do* much of the actual work. A useful metaphor is that of a baseball manager. The baseball manager is responsible for all that is happening in the game and on the field. They make the important decisions of which players to start the game, what the batting order should be, when the pitcher needs a pep talk, who and when to relieve the pitcher, and who to substitute toward the end of the game to pinch run, bunt, or pinch hit.

The baseball manager is not responsible for batting, pitching, or fielding directly; the manager does not play in the game; the manager must rely on others to get the job done. The manager watches the game closely, makes important decisions to improve their team's chances of winning throughout the course of the game, and tries to positively change the outcome of the game as it happens. Prior to the game, the manager also coaches the team to verify that the skills and behaviors or actions for success are routinely practiced.

So what does a school superintendent *really* do? Similar to the metaphor of the baseball manager, much of the work involves facilitating, motivating, relying on, and following through with the people that work in the district under the direct supervision of the superintendent. Setting the goals, focus, and tone for their districts, superintendents need to provide clarity for what they expect of their respective leadership team members. They need to provide support when necessary, assist team members in overcoming barriers to higher levels of performance and, at times, provide reasoning and rationale regarding the importance of the work to others.

Maybe twenty to thirty years ago, principals could operate primarily as building managers and be perceived as effective, or least get by. But not anymore. School principals need to be educational leaders, and superintendents need to verify that their principals model instructional leadership.

LEADING FOR INSTRUCTIONAL IMPROVEMENT

Even though the brunt of the work will ultimately be implemented through others, there are a number of ways the superintendent can, and should, lead instructional improvements. The following are some practical strategies for the school superintendent to positively influence and keep the focus on teaching and learning:

- Organize your meetings so that teaching and learning are the top priorities.
- Conduct focused learning walks with principal leadership teams, asking principals what they saw and how they would coach teachers for improvement.
- Check that school board agendas *always* include a focus on teaching and learning.
- Provide a mentor or coach for your principals who may need assistance with instructional leadership practices.
- Create and revisit your district strategic plan to highlight a focus on teaching and learning.
- Align budget priorities to teaching and learning initiatives.
- Celebrate student and staff successes around teaching and learning priorities.

Organize Meetings to Make Teaching and Learning the Top Priorities

In planning agendas when meeting with your school principals, school board, and any other groups that you are responsible to lead, structure your time to focus on teaching and learning. Taking your eye off the prize in leading instructional improvements may inadvertently make you negligent in your job responsibilities. Even if the work will flow through others, the school superintendent must assist principals with goal setting, monitor school improvement plans, and hold people accountable to make improvements in teaching and learning.

There may be political difficulties with a well-respected or veteran principal who doesn't prioritize teaching and learning—especially if you are a new superintendent. It is important to not let up and not allow certain individuals to derail or ignore your educational initiatives.

No one should sabotage your efforts. Make personnel decisions that put instructional leaders in positions of influence. Plan meetings accordingly so that everyone knows your mission.

Conduct Focused Learning Walks with Principal Leadership Teams

Learning walks get school superintendents into classrooms with their principals. This not only conveys unity—it also conveys that what is happening in the classroom is important. When conducting walkthroughs, there should be specific look-fors or processes in place to see whether certain instructional initiatives or improvements are in play.

It would be wise to utilize walkthrough protocols when conducting learning walks. Even if the superintendent–school principal classroom walkthroughs are nonevaluative in nature, what is seen (or perhaps *not* seen) should lead to conversations between the school superintendent and the principal that reference district plans and school improvement goals related to improving instruction and learning experiences for students.

It is also important to clarify the purpose of the learning walk. As school superintendent, you are likely to have opinions about what you see when you walk into a classroom. While you may be tempted to share with the building principal your long list of how a teacher might improve the learning experience, you may want to reconsider.

As superintendent, you are responsible for principals. Their skills, or lack thereof, when engaging with teachers around instructional improvement will have a deeper impact on improvement than you will. You should use these learning walks as a time to hear how the principal will coach the teacher. You should use this opportunity to coach your principal on how to leverage walkthroughs for improved learning, not to demonstrate your deep knowledge of teaching and learning.

Check That School Board Agendas Always Focus on Teaching and Learning

Keeping the school board in the loop is important, especially when it comes to garnering their support to use funds for certain programs, purchases, or initiatives. As superintendent, you should include updates related to teaching and learning initiatives in your biweekly or monthly school superintendent updates at public school board meetings.

When others have more knowledge or expertise in certain areas, or when you want to highlight specific programs, you should empower your assistant superintendent for teaching and learning/curriculum content leaders to provide these updates. You also can facilitate teaching and learning subcommittees with your school board to allow them a voice or a chance to participate in some of your district processes.

Provide a Coach for Principals Needing Assistance with Instructional Leadership Practices

In addition to your guidance and support for your principals, you might consider providing a more formal coach for any building-based leaders who may need assistance with leading instructional improvements within their schools. Principals are so busy in their day-to-day school-based operations, and they often need someone besides their boss to provide them with candid, yet non-judgmental feedback to help them grow.

Create and Revisit Your District Strategic Plan to Highlight a Focus on Teaching and Learning

Teaching and learning should be the focus of any district strategic plan, and the district plan should be revisited at least a few times a year so that it does not sit on a shelf but continues to drive instructional improvements. School improvement plans should align and flow from district plans, and teacher goals that include making efforts to improve instruction should align with school-based plans. Superintendents should create district plans that strive to improve teaching and learning initiatives, and then check to see whether their principals are implementing school-based plans that align with a similar focus.

Align Budget Priorities to Teaching and Learning Initiatives

Using the budget development process to leverage improvements to instruction is critical. Communication is key when it comes to how you plan presentations, and public discussions about how taxpayer money is being spent and will be spent in the future. The school board and the community at large will be more likely to support budgets that they can understand—budgets that enable educators to do things like make curricula improvements for students, lower class sizes, and provide support for all learners.

Superintendents need to ascertain that those who work to build the annual budget (business managers, assistant superintendents for finance, principals, and any other administrators who build budgets) know that any spending priorities must support instructional improvements for students. This includes adding new positions, purchasing materials, and providing professional development.

Remember to keep priorities straight when building a district budget. Superintendents may need to educate and "teach" some leadership team members how their budgets and spending practices need to align with instructional goals and priorities.

SUPERVISING AND EVALUATING PRINCIPALS AND LEADERSHIP TEAM MEMBERS

A responsibility of primary importance to the superintendent is coaching their school principals to be educational leaders. Superintendents can model what they expect of their principals and other leadership team members through biweekly leadership team meetings with set agendas that include opportunities for the principals and leadership team members to add topics to the agendas, learn together, collaborate, and move initiatives forward.

If school principals or leadership team members are deemed deficient in the realm of educational leadership after being given a fair amount of time to demonstrate proficiency by the school superintendent, it is the superintendent's responsibility to make changes in the school's leadership. Not making a change when one is needed makes a superintendent complicit in mediocrity. Typically, if a leadership team member is incapable of improving, despite your efforts to provide clarity and support, they are either incompetent or insubordinate—and neither trait is desirable.

Besides getting a *feeling* for whether a school principal or leadership team member that serves under a superintendent is making progress, superintendents can and should do any of the following:

- Conduct frequent school visits, which include making rounds and walking through classrooms with the principal, then listening to the principal discuss what they saw in terms of strengths and areas in need of improvement.
- Preview faculty meeting agendas that school principals set in advance of their faculty meetings, then sit in on some of the faculty meetings led by the principal.
- Help set and review annual principal or leadership team member goals, provide feedback for their goal setting as needed, and then hold quarterly meetings to check in on the progress regarding benchmarks or priority initiatives that were outlined in their goals.
- Ask leadership team members and principals to show you some of their observation write-ups of their teachers and staff to demonstrate how they are utilizing the educator evaluation process to leverage improvements to teaching and learning.
- Listen to staff members who provide unsolicited feedback to you about principals or other leadership team members, always respecting boundaries of roles.
- With school board support, reward highly effective leadership team members or principals with contract extensions or raises.

- As previously mentioned, if needed, make changes in personnel in a forthright and respectful manner.

SETTING THE TONE

As stated earlier, how we supervise and evaluate principals and leadership team members matters. It also matters how you go about doing it. Just as you want to be treated with respect by your school board, your leadership team members and school principals want to be treated with respect by *you*. Perhaps you have worked for a difficult superintendent or a supervisor who belittled others in the past. Or maybe you have worked with someone who made it obvious through their words, actions, or body language that they disliked or disapproved of certain people as subordinates. It is not right for a superintendent to act this way.

Even in the presence of someone who demonstrates incompetence, insubordination, mediocrity, or betrayal, superintendents should model how to treat others with respect and dignity. Leadership team members will talk with others about how they are treated by their superintendents. They want to work for someone who is a good person, but also someone who makes them a better leader.

Think of the best teacher you have had. Chances are the best teacher was not the one who doled out the easy A. Or the one who was overly nice, with low expectations. Or the one who was too strict and didn't seem to care about you as a person.

Your best teacher was likely someone that tried to get to know you, had high expectations of you, and tried to make you better. This is the type of superintendent people want to work for. It can be a difficult balance, but one—when struck—that will support success.

Superintendents need to model what they expect of their leadership team members. You want your educators, principals, and leadership team members to be kind to students, staff, and families. So be kind to your team. You want your people to be prepared, so do the same for your leadership team by building meaningful leadership team meeting agendas that focus on teaching and learning.

You want your school principals to have high expectations of their staff and students, so be sure to follow up on your expectations for success with your leadership team members and principals. Hold them accountable, but also try to provide them with appropriate resources and support. You don't want your people to make excuses, so don't make excuses yourself.

Allow Others Autonomy

Just as a school superintendent does not want to be micromanaged by their school board, principals and other leadership team members do not want to be micromanaged or suffocated by their superintendent. People need space from constant oversight to do their best work. Superintendents need to create supportive *conditions* for people to do their best work.

A superintendent's influence on improving what happens in the classroom is through the building principals. Therefore, superintendents should *empower* school principals by allowing them independence and support to do their best work without constraints or fear of making mistakes. Superintendents should be ready to provide guidance and mentorship for their principals without always telling them exactly what to do.

Whether good or bad, school principals need to be able to make their own decisions and have the autonomy and confidence from their superintendent to subsequently deal with the consequences or outcomes of those decisions, positive or negative. Too often principals may make decisions to try to please or appease their superintendent as their supervisor because the superintendent has overstepped and directed them precisely on what to do. At times this may be necessary; for example, a superintendent may need to make the decision to close a school due to a newly discovered safety hazard. But it usually isn't necessary for a superintendent to direct a principal using a top-down approach.

What's worse than a principal following orders from above is when a superintendent takes credit for a principal's decision or work, or if a principal is perceived as rudderless or powerless because they have told others that a decision was made because the superintendent has told them to do so. There is nothing wrong with implementing and following a chain of command, but principals should be able to do their jobs without oversight that may hinder their autonomy, authority, or leadership.

The following are some examples of how a superintendent can undermine a principal's authority:

- Meeting with department heads and/or individual teachers without the principal being present or at least aware of the purpose of the meeting
- Telling a principal which teachers or staff members they should hire or terminate
- Walking through classrooms and critiquing teachers
- Selecting a program for a principal to implement in their school (which was not chosen as a district-wide program)

- Using the authority of the superintendency to grant requests of faculty and staff, outside the typical approval process that involves the school principal's first approval or denial

Let School Principals Do Their Own Hiring and Firing

A superintendent can empower principals by granting them the autonomy and authority to do their own hiring and firing. It is appropriate for superintendents to meet with teacher finalists to do a final screening and determine the salary scale, but superintendents should not be the ones who pick the people who will report to and work for the principals. Superintendents who trust their school principals should allow their building leaders to hire their own staff and pick their own new teachers.

This does not mean that you as the superintendent should not meet with finalist candidates or blindly accept principal recommendations for hire. You should always screen and meet with teachers and educators that principals want to hire to make sure they are the right people to work with your students, and to talk about how their educational philosophies align with your district's mission and vision.

The hiring process is just much smoother if, prior to hiring new staff, your principals' and hiring managers' beliefs, leadership styles, and educational philosophies already match yours as the superintendent. Effective school superintendents will coach their principals or hiring managers on how to screen applications, conduct interviews, and check references when talking to finalist candidates' supervisors.

IT'S NOT JUST THE PRINCIPALS AND TEACHERS

Think about who else can help—for example, paraprofessionals or teacher assistants are very important people in the lives of our students. What professional development opportunities can we lead, facilitate, or provide for paraprofessionals to assist in their growth? What about our custodians and maintenance workers, administrative assistants, and central office staff? How do we include them in highlighting how important their work is to contributing to our educators' teaching and our students' learning?

Who else in addition to your principals, teachers, paraprofessionals, and other staff need to know that teaching and learning is your focus? Parents are integral, so we need to make sure that our principals, and also us as superintendents, highlight exciting teaching and learning happening in our communications. And students are our most important clients, so we need to be sure to include our students when talking about what initiatives are being planned and happening in our schools.

LESSONS ABOUT THE IMPORTANCE OF KEEPING A HYPERFOCUS ON TEACHING AND LEARNING

There will be many opportunities to lose focus on teaching and learning, just as there will be many threats to derail teaching and learning initiatives. For example, people will try to get you to ban books, ignore state mandates, or change your budget priorities.

General political pressures may overwhelm your days as you respond and manage these situations. If you succumb too easily to distractions and pressures, you will potentially ignore big-picture responsibilities, which may lead others to assume they can detract you from focusing on leading what is most important—improving teaching and learning.

People are watching. If community members and those who serve under you observe your volition wane, and they perceive you are losing your laser-like focus on teaching and learning, you are unlikely to have the impact that you want, and students need. After all, how will your principals, building leaders, and teachers implement important teaching and learning initiatives if their school superintendent is willing to put these initiatives on the back burner, or change course when there is pressure to do less?

Stay Close to the Classrooms

Spending time where the action happens is integral to staying focused on teaching and learning. There is nothing more important than what happens in the classroom between the student and the teacher.

The following are a few strategies you might consider in order to stay close to where the important work is taking place:

- Participate in student shadow experiences to witness firsthand any successes or shortcomings of the school day.
- Conduct a "residency" at each school and use a hallway desk so that people have access to you.
- Attend and participate in professional development with teachers.
- Avoid the trap and comfort of the superintendent's office and deliberately schedule regular time in schools where the teaching and learning is happening.

- Meet with student advisory groups, teacher groups, and parent groups to gain authentic perceptions about the teaching and learning happening within the school district.

CONCLUSION

In trying to keep teaching and learning the main priority, superintendents always need to look to improving students' learning experiences in the schools, which ultimately should boost student achievement. Remembering their roots as an educator, it is of the utmost importance for the superintendent of schools to look to lead instructional improvements and advancements. This can be done through the superintendent keeping their priorities straight and motivating others to always keep the focus on teaching and learning.

Superintendents can organize the district leadership team meetings they lead, conduct focused learning walks alongside principals, and verify that school board meeting agendas always include a focus on teaching and learning. Superintendents can also support their building leaders by providing coaches for any principals who may need assistance with instructional leadership.

District strategic plans and school-based improvement plans should be created and revisited to support innovative teaching and learning practices. Budget priorities should also be directly related to teaching and learning initiatives.

Lastly, it is important to note that building leaders serve as an extension of the district superintendent. *Who* is in place in each position matters. Superintendents need to bravely supervise and evaluate principals and leadership team members, providing autonomy and support for their team members, yet also setting the tone that what is truly best for all students is to keep a laser-like focus on improving teaching and learning practices. And to uphold high expectations and avoid mediocrity or complacency, the school superintendent must address those who do not adhere to this mindset.

EXPERIENCES FROM THE FIELD

Not focusing on teaching and learning will derail any superintendent. A superintendent we know was hired to a district because of his financial acumen and good track record as a business manager. Despite him continuing to do what he had done well in previous districts, he was not well-regarded in his new district. His demise was due to staying away from teaching and learning initiatives, and he communicated that he "didn't want to get in the way" of the teachers. Although this mindset may have been somewhat refreshing to some educators, he was ultimately just viewed as a numbers guy, or someone who didn't care, or was out of touch with the teaching and learning happening in the district.

Leading for instructional improvement should motivate any school superintendent. We can always improve, and although others within the school district will be more intimately involved than the superintendent in teaching and learning initiatives, the school superintendent is the one who needs to lead the charge with their leadership team, school board(s), and community. Improving teaching and learning experiences for students should be the focus for any superintendent.

ADDITIONAL RESOURCES

D'Auria, John P., and Paul B. Ash. *School Systems That Learn: Improving Professional Practice, Overcoming Limitations, and Diffusing Innovation*. Thousand Oaks, CA: SAGE Publications, 2012.

Fink, S., and A. Markholt. *Leading for Instructional Improvement: How Successful Leaders Develop Teaching and Learning Expertise*. San Francisco: Jossey-Bass, 2011.

"Learning Walks: A Portal to Strengthening Practice." ELAchieve. Accessed January 1, 2022. https://www.elachieve.org/blog/learning-walks-portal-strengthening-practice/.

Chapter 3

Making New Friends

Nurturing Relationships with School Board Members

EXPERIENCES FROM THE FIELD

I remember when I first started as superintendent. I was unsure about how to work with my school board. I waited for them to call me with questions or issues. I was scared of what they might say or ask of me at public school committee meetings.

In thinking back, I was more reactive than proactive as a new superintendent. As I began to speak to other superintendents about how they worked with their school boards, I learned that the more effective superintendents didn't just react—they took charge of how they handled sharing information with their school boards in the time between their bimonthly public school board meetings.

They met and spoke to their individual school board members somewhat routinely. They had phone conversations, texted them with brief updates that needed to be shared immediately, and conducted informal personal meetings to just talk, answer questions, and foster relationships with their school board members. They were able to build a strong and collaborative relationship with their school board members.

RELATIONSHIPS, RELATIONSHIPS, RELATIONSHIPS

Just like the three most important things in real estate are *location, location, location*, the three most important things for a new superintendent are *relationships, relationships, relationships*. A superintendent can be effective and accomplish almost anything with the confidence, support, and faith of their local school board and other key constituents they serve. Not much meaningful work will get done unless the superintendent builds solid relationships with their administrators, teachers, parents, and students.

School board members should also be included in a superintendent's relationship building. After all, school board members are the people who will ultimately vote to move the critical work of a school district forward to do great things for students. It is important for you to purposefully develop strong relationships with school board members.

DEVELOPING AND MAINTAINING PRODUCTIVE RELATIONS WITH YOUR BOARD

A key to the success of any relationship is developing, nurturing, and maintaining a caring and positive relationship. This chapter explores and reiterates the importance of the superintendent relationship with school board members, both collectively and individually. It also shares specific strategies a superintendent can use to develop positive relations with other city or town officials besides the school board members.

While the superintendent is hired to manage and lead the day-to-day operations of the school district, the members of the school board are active and engaged partners in this work who cannot be overlooked or undervalued. It is critical that the superintendent recognize and allow school board members to be active and respected partners in the work.

An important first step for the superintendent is to make it a priority to develop collaborative and positive relationships that support engaging in sincere and honest conversations with school board members. The development of positive relationships will help you garner support for important work related to improving teaching and learning within the school district. A strong relationship will also serve you well in many other situations, such as when a crisis occurs that impacts the district.

The relationship between the superintendent and the school board should be one of mutual respect. Confidence is built over time when a trusting relationship becomes established. There should be no surprises or hidden information between the superintendent and the school board. Both sides should try to be transparent.

A strong relationship between the superintendent and the school board is tantamount to your longevity and success. Communicating early and often with school board members will build confidence and credibility. A healthy school superintendent/school board relationship will help both a school superintendent and their school board build leadership capacity and accomplish goals in the school district they lead.

Make It Personal

In most communities, members of the school board are elected community members who receive minimal or no compensation for their work on the school board. Every school board member makes the personal decision to run for this elected office because of goals that they hope to achieve. As you begin to build relationships with school board members, it is important to understand the underlying motivation that moved them to run for their elected position, or at least express interest in the role of school board member if they were appointed.

It is likely that some members of the school board will be upfront and transparent about their motivation and goals. Other members may be less willing to share their motivation for wanting to be on the school board. If possible, you may want to review videos of debates, or news stories, from when each board member ran for office. Whether elected or appointed, it is important for the superintendent to learn about the individual motivations or desires of each member on the school board, and to identify opportunities to support them in achieving their goals where appropriate and in alignment with district and school goals.

The Importance of Regular In-Person Meetings

A critical approach to developing strong relationships with anyone is to find time to meet and nurture individual relationships. Individual, in-person meetings can serve as a means to accelerate relationship building and ensure healthy relationships are fostered with every member of a school board. In these meetings, the improved familiarity will give individual members the opportunity to better know you as an individual, and in turn you better know them. This approach will support the building of trust between a superintendent and school board.

Most experts agree that at least 60–70 percent of in-person communication is nonverbal. Even though it may be more productive in terms of time management to meet virtually, or talk by phone, a superintendent should make sincere and repeated efforts to meet in person with school board members. When possible, you should have coffee at a local diner, meet somewhere for lunch, or schedule an early dinner before an evening you need to attend.

The out-of-office meeting will serve to create a more level playing field between the superintendent and school board members. It will also allow the superintendent to focus solely on that individual meeting, without any interruptions that might occur while meeting in the superintendent's office or school setting.

A superintendent's body language is important when conversing with and listening to any constituents, including school board members, while meeting in person. Making eye contact and showing empathy conveys interest and care. Not fiddling with or being distracted by your phone shows this time is valued and sacred.

Being honest and inquisitive also creates a culture of candor, respect, and inquiry. Finally, during these individual meetings with school board members, superintendents should engage in behaviors—both verbal and nonverbal—that continue to send the message that the meeting is important.

Talk Regularly with Individual Board Members

It is vitally important for the superintendent to talk regularly with individual school board members. For a superintendent in a regional school district with multiple school boards, or with school boards as big as nine or more individual members, it will obviously be more challenging to accomplish the goal of meeting consistently with every individual school board member. With that being said, a superintendent may need to have more phone calls or virtual meetings than in-person meetings with individual board members. Ask about their individual preferences.

Getting a sense of individual board members' thoughts, beliefs, intentions, and oftentimes personal agendas is critical to foreseeing potential opportunities for partnership, speed bumps, or landmines. Meeting with individual board members also allows the superintendent to learn more about supportive or disruptive parents, valuable community members, or other political activities happening internally within other city or town boards and committees.

Dealing with Dissension

According to Howard Carlson, when an individual board member expresses dissent, those "board members are opening from one of three paradigms: (1) The board member is unaware of the true facts related to the issue; (2) The individual is acting on the basis of strongly held philosophical beliefs; or (3) The board member is agenda-driven and thus is not participating in good faith."[1]

Although superintendents already have to deal with enough dissension and polarization in their roles, it is important to understand the primary reasons why individual school board members may be upset or divided from the rest of the school board. Individual members may want to be the next chairperson, or perhaps they were previously the school board chair and miss that more powerful role. If an individual school board member were to become the school board chair in the future, it is also especially important for you to help educate them in understanding how the process of being a school board chair functions.

WORKING WITH YOUR SCHOOL BOARD CHAIR

Meet Consistently with the Chair to Mutually Set School Board Meeting Agendas

Even more important than meeting with individual school board members is meeting frequently and routinely with the school board chair. While decisions are made by the majority of school committee members who are working as a whole, a school board chair has some responsibilities to act on behalf of the entire board. The school board chair should be in charge of leading and streamlining the communications with the school board, just as the superintendent is in charge of leading and streaming communications with district leaders and ultimately all school district personnel.

Meeting every two weeks, or more frequently, with your school board chair is important to maintaining cohesiveness and a focus on the overall mission. Having consistent biweekly meetings, prescheduled and committed to by both the superintendent and the school board chair, will foster collaborative conversations and collegial connections. These regular meetings will also ensure that the superintendent and school board chair stay focused on addressing the most important issues.

Meeting frequently will help the district leader and board leader take care of the small issues so they can be resolved in a timely manner before potentially becoming bigger problems. There will also be opportunities to identify ways to partner in order to deliberately share the political work of a district. In addition, potential new agenda items can be discussed or debated before deciding whether to place these items on the next school board meeting agenda.

Biweekly or at least monthly meetings between the superintendent and school board chair ensures that, as matters arise that may need to be addressed throughout the year, a superintendent can have the opportunity at least twice a month to problem-solve *prior* to public board meetings. Developing school board meeting agendas together with the chair indicates unity and demonstrates that the two leaders serve as a high-functioning team. Working together will also ensure that the superintendent's areas of responsibility that require school board approval or consent are added to agendas to meet required timelines.

When meeting biweekly with the school board chair, the superintendent can share challenges and successes that transpire with their hundreds (or thousands) of staff and thousands (or tens of thousands) of students. Conversely, the chair can share with the superintendent their own challenges and successes transpiring with the other individual school board members and the community at large. Perhaps the superintendent can also advise the school board chair on how to best proceed with future communications to other board members.

Besides setting the next school board meeting agenda together, there are likely other topics for the superintendent to discuss with the school board chair. Examples of topics to discuss could be strategizing for teacher contract negotiations, discussing superintendent or school district goals, planning future subcommittee or work sessions, or reviewing school board policies that may need to be revisited. In addition, the school superintendent or school board chair may want to foreshadow coming challenges, or simply discuss some issues percolating that the superintendent and school board chair want each other to be aware of.

Being on the same page with the school board chair can also help the superintendent make sure there are no surprises at school board meetings. It can be very helpful for a school board chair to give the superintendent a "heads-up" to prepare the superintendent for questions the chair plans to ask them in public at the next school board meeting.

The school board chair can also let the superintendent know particular questions they think other school board members may ask related to an agenda item. Subsequent to biweekly meetings between the superintendent and the school board chair, an effective and influential school board chair can help explain or "sell" the merits of a topic or initiative to other school board members. They might also ask specific questions to draw out a greater level of clarity, or to represent a question that might be on the minds of many.

Plan School Board Work Sessions That Focus on Student Achievement

Aside from subcommittees, a superintendent and school board chair should plan and engage in school board "work sessions." Work sessions can be conveniently scheduled before or after regular school board meetings. These sessions can be opportunities for a superintendent to educate or "teach" the school board members, who often are not educators themselves, about school-related work such as racial equity, diversity, and inclusivity training, or how a "Vision of a Graduate" is needed to articulate the specific competencies a high school graduate needs to be prepared for the real world as they leave our schools to begin college or career.

Work sessions will allow a superintendent and school board to have time to openly discuss mutual goals that should aim to improve the schools and ultimately lead to student successes. A superintendent can also invite internal or external consultants who may have certain expertise to assist with strategic planning or other specialized initiatives. Strategic goals discussed can be related to the goals of the superintendent, school board, or the entire school system. These goals can help to establish a three- to five-year strategic plan, or district strategy for continuous improvement, that will guide the future work in the school district.

CONVERSE AND COLLABORATE WITH OTHER CITY OR TOWN LEADERS

Much like a superintendent needs to be proactive in their outreach with school board members, a superintendent needs to use similar outreach strategies with other city or town leaders. This is important if you rely on those relationships to support funding for your district, and is especially important if your school board members do not have relationships with other town leaders.

Collaboration with community leaders outside of your school district should only strengthen support for the students and school board you serve. The relationship between the school district and other town boards and key local constituents needs to be productive. The school superintendent needs to be proactive and collaborative with local leaders outside of the school board in order to enhance the experiences of students.

As you likely know, a superintendent needs to anticipate that they must sometimes swim in their city's or town's political waters, and also deal with political issues—some overt and others more covert and often nuanced. A school superintendent may need to *navigate, advocate, or mediate* in this capacity. While navigating choppy seas, superintendents should stay focused on building capacity to lead systemic change to improve the school system. These broad challenges offer another opportunity to partner with school board members for assistance.

A school superintendent should be transparent and accessible to other city or town leaders. A superintendent who attends other board meetings aside from their own school board meetings is seen and heard by new constituents. It may be a change for elected officials or community members to see the district superintendent at community meetings outside of school board meetings or school events.

If a superintendent goes out of their way to collaborate with other local leaders, this should be welcomed by fellow city or town leaders. Other community leaders will appreciate a superintendent being there, showing they care, and being accessible. Superintendents should, of course, do this in tandem with the school board chair, or at least make the chair aware of this outreach so the chair does not feel slighted or less involved than the superintendent. Collaboration is always key.

With a school system's budget typically consuming anywhere between 40 percent and 60 percent of a city's or town's overall spending, a superintendent should ensure transparency so that elected and appointed officials know how this money is being spent. At least annually, the superintendent should share and communicate school district priorities, publish a budget calendar, and then align the school system budget goals to match priority initiatives. Educational needs and rationales should be communicated, such as prioritizing the need to reduce class sizes, make facilities improvements, or upgrade technology. Ideally, this will occur through a presentation at the meetings of other boards.

In addition, the superintendent should write, publish, and share with other city and town leaders—and the broader community—a budget narrative to advocate for funding and summarize how school department monies are spent. This budget narrative should not be more than eight or ten pages (we have seen some as long as a hundred pages!) because lay people will not read the document if it is too long. If a longer narrative is necessary, a short executive summary may be helpful.

The budget narrative should tell a story about how the budget will improve the school experience for children. The superintendent should embed links to documents, data, visuals, and other information in the budget narrative in order to make the needs of the schools clear and understandable to the general public.

With the school board chair, a superintendent should have quarterly meetings with community leaders such as the city or town council chair and the mayor or town manager/administrator. The superintendent should also meet annually with the city's or town's capital improvement committee to share facilities needs and seek feedback before publishing a revised three- to five-year school department plan to maintain or enhance the physical plant at each school campus.

Failure to do this at least yearly will result in school buildings and facilities being overlooked or neglected. Another group to meet with at least annually is the FinCom (finance committee), which typically serves in an advisory capacity to recommend spending—or recommend not spending—on certain city or town projects.

Collaboration with municipal leaders on key initiatives that will benefit both the city or town and the students and staff in the schools is tantamount to the success of a school superintendent. School board members usually talk to other local leaders, and they may hear positive things about a superintendent from others in town, which will enhance the perception of the superintendent's competence.

The community at large will view the superintendent and other local leaders advocating and planning for funding together to meet the schools' needs as a very positive thing. Conversely, a school superintendent having a nonexistent or dysfunctional relationship with municipal leaders will not last long in that city or town.

COMMUNICATE IN A VARIETY OF WAYS

A superintendent should use a variety of tools to communicate with the school board and also with the community at large. Group texts are an efficient way for a superintendent to share news for informational purposes only with their school board, such as quickly informing the board of an accident involving a student, letting board members know about a disturbance at a school (if an ambulance needs to transport an injured student or a student in crisis), or announcing an upcoming new administrator hire right before a press release goes out.

Individual school board members may often field questions about school news ahead of the superintendent or aside from the superintendent's office. Therefore, it is important for the school board to hear about noteworthy school-related events in a timely manner directly from the superintendent, especially since board members are typically more accessible to community members than the superintendent of schools. School superintendents usually will need some time to manage a crisis situation and then craft a thoughtful message prior to giving detailed information to the community.

In the twenty-first century, a superintendent should seriously consider employing a reputable public relations firm to assist with messaging. Besides dealing with unexpected crises, public relations experts can quickly and professionally help a superintendent or school board craft succinct communications to highlight positive school news, celebrate achievements, and help the community to see and learn about school and district accomplishments.

If a superintendent crafts weekly or biweekly electronic written updates to send to the school board, with easily accessible visual images and links detailing information related to education and the school system, it will convey professionalism and build confidence in the superintendent as an effective communicator.

Although email still seems to be the primary mode of communication, texting, calling, utilizing social media, and meeting in person are important components for community members to see the superintendent and school board as accessible and established entities.

MANAGE RELATIONSHIPS CAREFULLY AND REMIND PEOPLE OF THEIR ROLES

A focus of this chapter has been on the importance of building a strong relationship with the school board. Through this strong relationship, a superintendent will be able to leverage the shared vision to accelerate achievement of the established goals. It is important to note, however, that a superintendent must develop, nurture, and manage these relationships carefully.

With a willingness to engage in regular open communication with school board members, and understand their individual motivations for running for these elected positions, there is a potential pitfall. The role and responsibility of the school superintendent and the school board is typically articulated in state law. As a superintendent works to develop a strong relationship with school board members, some members may misinterpret their role and responsibility and begin to assume authority in areas that are in the purview of the superintendent. They may, for example, believe that they can act individually on behalf of the entire school board.

The school board is an elected body that has authority only when constituted as a body, and when meeting in public. In these instances, the superintendent must carefully and tactfully provide clarity on role responsibility. Failure to do so will likely lead to situations where a school board member has assumed authority that is the responsibility of the school superintendent. Or an individual member may believe that they are acting on behalf of the entire school board.

Redirecting a member of the school board can be a challenging situation, but with the development of a strong relationship, these difficult conversations are much easier. Making these corrections can be difficult, but it is necessary to create understanding and tacit agreement around role clarity.

SHOULD I STAY OR SHOULD I GO?

Should things go badly and the school superintendent–school board relationship deteriorates to the point where it is a public distraction to the community, it may be time for the superintendent to think about leaving. All superintendents should strive to establish longevity in their roles; however, there may be times when the school superintendent–school board relationship is toxic, or the superintendent feels they are not supported by their school board. When this happens, it may be time for the superintendent to pursue other educational leadership positions in different school districts.

If the superintendent truly strives to do what is best for kids, and what's best for the school district, it is probably not beneficial to student learning for the superintendent to stay in a dysfunctional relationship with their school board that is beyond repair.

CONCLUSION

This chapter outlines some key actions that superintendents can take to maximize productivity while fostering positive relationships with their school board in order to achieve mutual goals and meet the needs of students in your school district. These action steps include the following:

- Hold in-person meetings.
- Meet frequently with the school board chair to collaborate as a team and set school board meeting agendas.
- Talk regularly with all individual board members.
- Converse with other city and town leaders.
- Plan work sessions that focus on goals related to student achievement.
- Communicate in a variety of ways.

EXPERIENCES FROM THE FIELD

Thinking back to whenever there has been confusion or miscommunication between myself and school board members, it has always been when I have not communicated frequently with individual board members. When there is a lull in communication, people can start to make assumptions only based on what they know, or don't know.

Meeting in person with board members allows me to consistently give them progress reports, updates, and a "heads-up" on various situations. Similarly, town or city leaders appreciate school district updates from the superintendent. Information sharing builds trust and a culture of care. I have never regretted sharing pertinent information in a transparent way with board members or other local constituents.

ADDITIONAL RESOURCES

Adamson, Michael T., and Bradley V. Balch. *Building Great School Board–Superintendent Teams: A Systematic Approach to Balancing Roles and Responsibilities.* Bloomington, IN: Solution Tree, 2017.

"Community Relations: A Key to Superintendent Success." Massachusetts Association of School Superintendents. Accessed January 2, 2023. https://www.massupt.org/2018/05/22/community-relations-a-key-to-superintendent-success/.

Townsend, R., G. Johnston, G. Gross, P. Lynch, L. Garcy, B. Roberts, and P. Novotney. *Effective Superintendent–School Board Practices: Strategies for Developing and Maintaining Good Relationships with Your Board*. Thousand Oaks, CA: Corwin, 2007.

Van Deuren, Amy E., Thomas F. Evert, and Bette A. Lang. *Working Toward Success: Board and Superintendent Interactions, Relationships, and Hiring Issues*. Lanham, MD: Rowman & Littlefield, 2016.

Chapter 4

Show Me the Money!

Budget Development to Improve Student Learning

EXPERIENCES FROM THE FIELD

In my first year as superintendent, my new role was overwhelming. Daily, I was dealing with a deluge of urgent matters that required my attention, while trying to learn the complexities of this new position. The first budget season was a blur, and we followed the district's previously practiced path to deliver a budget recommendation to the school board that met expected parameters. Following the approval of the budget by both the school board and town council, I had cleared time to work with the business manager to talk about how we would implement the budget.

I realized that an important educational initiative was not funded, which included after-school tutoring and mentoring of identified struggling learners. This missed opportunity served as a lesson learned: I had to be sure to use the budget process to impact student learning. From that moment on, I have approached every budget development process as an opportunity to improve the outcomes for our students.

THE WORLD OF SCHOOL FINANCE

The budget process is often the great unknown for a new superintendent. Since the majority of new superintendents progressed through a traditional educational career pathway to land their first superintendent position, they usually have had little formal experience or training with school finance—except perhaps the one graduate class to become licensed. While the traditional career path—teacher, principal, assistant superintendent,

superintendent—will support your success as a superintendent, your lack of school finance acumen will hinder that success.

This chapter explores the importance of developing competency and credibility with the district's budget and the budget development process. Specifically, this chapter will outline how a superintendent can hone their skills utilizing the budget process to impact student learning.

Getting Familiar with the District Budget

A district's budget is a multimillion-dollar proposition—and you are now in charge of it! With many complicated revenue streams and expenses, it is often difficult to gain an understanding of the mechanics of the budget, the process to develop the annual budget and, most importantly, how you can leverage your deep understanding of the budget to fund initiatives connected to enhanced learning opportunities for improved student outcomes.

There are many skills a superintendent must possess to find success. The ability to understand and leverage the budget process to support student learning is often overlooked. It is typical that new superintendents look at school finance as a technical process that does not easily lend itself to creativity and innovation for students. This sentiment could not be further from the truth. As a new superintendent, you must approach the development of the budget as an adaptive challenge.

So how does a school superintendent gain the knowledge and skills to leverage the district budget for students, while also ensuring that the district does not go bankrupt? The superintendent must develop a deliberate professional learning plan to ensure success in this area, with an eye toward identifying opportunities to make changes and improve student learning. An effective superintendent needs to think about who to include in the budget development process, ways to improve the budget process, strategies to build consensus among stakeholders, and how to gain public support for the eventual approval of the budget. The plan should include the following:

- Understanding the district budget
- Initiating a budget development process
- Presenting and "selling" your annual budget
- Ensuring budget initiatives are meeting expectations

As is true in many aspects of our work, urgency drives our attention. As we know, however, those urgent items may not actually be the most important. One way to protect against moving from urgent issue to urgent issue, or crisis to crisis, without tackling the most meaningful work is to develop a plan to complete a comprehensive budget development process. If you do not develop a clear plan, the imperative to pay attention to the budget process may not happen, and in turn could have a detrimental impact on student learning. Early in your tenure, leveraging the budget should be seen as an opportunity to provide the children in your district with improved learning opportunities.

The Multimillion-Dollar Puzzle

School finance is complicated—like, really complicated. School funding approaches vary across the nation, but typically are some combination of local, state, and federal sources. Funding comes in the form of local contributions, state contributions, state and federal entitlement and competitive grants, as well as other sources. Each source of funding has different and specific rules and requirements for use that further confuse superintendents and complicate the budget process. Through this complexity, all of these pieces must come together to support the district's primary mission.

An important early goal of any new superintendent is to begin to develop an understanding of the district budget. This is both a technical and adaptive task. The good news is that your district employs a skilled professional who has built their career on understanding the complexity of school finance—the director of finance (or school business administrator).

Your director of finance, business officer, school business administrator, chief financial officer, assistant superintendent—or whatever title they are known by—should be someone you bring coffee to and plan to meet with regularly. Develop them as a partner and ally in this important work. After all, it is this individual who holds the key to your deep learning around school finance.

There is an important caveat, however—you must be sure to approach this relationship carefully. Your failure to effectively articulate your purpose and goals to the director of finance may lead to feelings of concern or resentment, or unintentionally signal your mistrust in this person. It is important for you to proactively work to avoid this possibility.

You must carefully develop a partnership where you share your goals with this individual and help them understand the important role they play in your fiscal education. You should enter this conversation thoughtfully and carefully, and with as much knowledge about past practices as possible. You may be walking into a situation where your predecessor never sought the advice of the director of finance, but only connected with them on the technical aspects of the budget; or you may be walking into a situation where the director of finance has been allowed to make all of the important financial decisions, without an eye toward educational improvement, and without input from the superintendent.

In the end, your approach will likely represent a change that could raise concern with the director of finance. Ultimately, your honest and transparent engagement with the director of finance will be key to ensuring a trusting relationship, a clear understanding of your goals around the school district's budget, and an awareness of their role in your financial education. As you enter the district, your goals with the director of finance should include the following:

- Gaining a deep understanding of your district's budget. What are the strengths and vulnerabilities of the budget? Where are you annually underfunded and overfunded? Are there major initiatives that have not been properly funded?
- Improving your understanding of the technical aspects of district funding, revenues, and expenditures. What are the sources of revenue and what are the rules to use those revenues? What are those areas where you have control? Is the district maximizing receipt of all available funds through grant processes?
- Identifying areas that require deeper analysis. What areas of the budget are still unclear? What areas of the budget are not reasonable?
- Initiating planning for cost-reduction or income-generation activities. What can you do to lower costs or raise revenues to support new educational initiatives?

With the help of your director of finance, your financial education will be on the fast track. This new understanding of district finances will give you the tools necessary to identify where opportunities for change live within the budget.

THE BUDGET DEVELOPMENT PROCESS

Before you wade into the budget development waters, it is important to understand the traditions and approaches that have existed within your community. It is also important for you to understand the intention and purpose—both stated and unstated—of these existing processes. Once you have gained that understanding, you can plan a budget development process that will combine those pre-existing traditions and approaches with your current approach to budget development.

As your first year begins, things will move quickly. The budget development process is an incredibly complicated and time-consuming task, with a deadline typically only months into your first year. An important element of the budget development process is to draft a roadmap that leads to the big event—presentation of your recommended budget. By starting with that date in mind, and working backward, you can put together a budget development process and a timeline that are thoughtful and deliberate.

There are four major components to the budget development process that must be carefully planned so that the time needed will be available:

1. Creating a budget development timeline/calendar
2. Identifying budget priorities with the leadership team
3. Developing the budget proposal with stakeholder engagement, including your school board
4. Selling the budget

Creating a Budget Development Timeline/Calendar

You must be organized, transparent, and clear as you embark on your budget development process. The development and sharing of a budget development timeline/calendar with key staff will serve to provide necessary transparency in the process, while also holding you accountable to accomplish each task. See table 4.1 for an example of a budget calendar that can be drafted and then published and shared with the community in late summer or early fall.

Identifying Budget Priorities with the Leadership Team

How will you identify the budget priorities? What will these priorities say about the values of the district? How will you evaluate existing initiatives so that your efforts continue to meet the needs of the district?

The identification of budget priorities is an important step in ensuring a budget that is developed around student needs. The task of developing budget priorities, together with your district leadership team, will send a very clear signal about your values. It will reiterate that you do not view this process as perfunctory, but rather one in which the deliberate planning and decision making of the district leadership team can have the power to positively change the lives of children.

We recommend that you approach this task without the influence of the anticipated budget projection. In many districts, the annual budget discussion is full of doom and gloom. There will never be enough resources to accomplish all of the goals. However, engaging in budget planning from the perspective of predetermined funding increases will have a determinantal and limiting effect, and could also result in members of the leadership team not sharing what actions you might take to most significantly impact student learning.

Table 4.1 Sample Budget Development Timeline

Timeline	Action Taken
September 27	School committee reviews FY24 budget development timeline
October 18	School committee advises administration regarding budget development target (needs-based, level-service, zero-based, level-funded, etc.) and approves FY24 budget calendar (if necessary)
October 18	Superintendent facilitates budget development discussion with district leadership team and school principals
November 8	Budget preparation package/instructions communicated to school principals and district administrators; budget priorities determined based on data analysis
November 8–December 17	School administrators/designated school and district staff prepare school budgets
December 15	Leadership team develops funding priorities with rationale
January 3–7	Budget meetings with individual principals/school administrators
January 5	Deadline for budget (staffing and expenses) requests to be returned to school superintendent and director of finance
January 5–10	Superintendent reviews budget proposals
January 13	School committee work session; FY24 budget priority discussion
January 31	Revenue estimates received by the state; governor's proposed budget
February 21	Superintendent finalizes FY24 budget recommendation
March 7	School committee public hearing and discussion of the superintendent's recommended FY24 budget
March 7	For annual town meeting, school committee finalizes FY24 recommended budget document
March 8	Budget documents posted on school district website and shared
March 15	Finance committee liaison meeting; budget documents distributed to finance committee in advance of meeting
March 17	Select board meeting; budget document distributed to select board in advance of meeting
March 21	School committee votes to approve FY24 budget
May 9	Budget presentation to town meeting by the mayor/town administrator and superintendent

The budget development process is just that, a process—when all the ideas have been shared, you can go back and review the budget to make decisions around reductions to align with school committee and community expectations.

You should approach the budget priority setting process with your leadership team as a kind of wish list. Ask your leadership team members to consider how to improve the experience and outcomes for students without worrying about the budget challenges. Push them to challenge conventional thinking and the long-established practices that continue year after year in your schools, whether or not they are successful. The goal is to come up with a short list of budget priorities that will directly connect to the student experience, and positively impact outcomes.

With that list, and the leadership team's buy-in on these priorities, you can engage the budget process in the framework of what is possible, rather than what is impossible. This approach will change the perspective of your leadership team members. They will be more engaged and invested in the agreed-on budget priorities. This commitment will give them permission to look at all aspects of their school's budget to determine whether they can offer any changes to make room for these priorities.

Connected to the development of a list of possible new initiatives and approaches, the leadership team should also review existing programs. A deep and deliberate review of existing programs and initiatives to assess effectiveness will provide the leadership team with opportunities to identify those initiatives that can be improved by leadership intervention, while also examining initiatives that might no longer provide the educational benefit anticipated when first implemented.

Once identified, the latter can then become part of a discussion about whether these pre-existing but underperforming initiatives should continue, or could be eliminated to create budget space for the new priorities identified by the leadership team.

The harsh reality is that it will likely be difficult to accomplish many of your budget priorities because of the constraints on school budgets across the nation. It is important to remember that the improvement of the district is a multiyear endeavor, with each year providing you with new opportunities to embed your budget priorities. Moreover, without a clearly understood and agreed-on set of budget priorities, you will likely miss opportunities for unexpected funding sources. With a plan and purpose in hand, you are able to seek out and capitalize on new opportunities as they arise.

Developing the Budget Proposal with Stakeholder Engagement

Who are you going to engage as part of the development process? Will you expand engagement to ensure that you hear the voices of many groups? Will faculty and staff have the opportunity to offer feedback? What process will you use to gather and analyze feedback?

The answers to these questions are important when enacting a budget development strategy that is collaborative and inclusive. A well-thought-out and fully executed strategy will also build buy-in to the budget throughout the process. The hopeful side effect of this approach is broad support for your budget proposal.

There is typically a great deal of interest in the budget development process. Stakeholders include faculty and staff, parents, students, community members, school board members, and other elected officials. You must develop a deliberate approach to allow each stakeholder group to have an opportunity to learn about the status of the budget development process, as well as opportunities to offer insight and opinions about what should be prioritized.

To manage the multiple streams of feedback about budget development and priorities, you must plan ahead. Use of a budget development timeline/calendar, like the one shared in table 4.1, will ensure that you have included stakeholders in the process and have incorporated feedback into your planning.

With each stakeholder group, you need to determine how you will collect feedback about the budget. There are many ways to collect feedback, and plans can differ based on the stakeholder group. You might decide to conduct school visits and "office hours" to hear feedback from faculty and staff, as well as offering them the opportunity to complete a survey to share ideas. To gather community feedback, you may choose to provide informal in-person meetings to allow the community to share feedback with you.

Whatever path you choose, it remains important to continue to provide transparent communication about the budget development process. Keep in mind that while you are collecting feedback on the priorities for budget development, you are also beginning the process of garnering support for your budget proposal.

Selling the Budget

Once you have a developed budget, with clearly articulated budget priorities, it is important to begin to gather support for your proposal within stakeholder groups and the broader community. While this happens with intention following the completion of the developed budget proposal, it is important to note that your work to gather feedback from stakeholders also represents building support for the budget proposal.

Too often, presentation of the budget becomes a technical process void of a deep understanding of the planned and intended impact on students. A budget proposal may be hundreds of pages of line items with dollar amounts that represent every planned expenditure by the district; a budget presentation may include dozens of slides that provide historical spending of highlighted accounts.

While this information is important, especially for the fiscal hawks in your community, this does not effectively communicate the budget proposal. Your budget presentation needs to tell the story. You need to answer the question for the community: *How will the expenditure of the proposed resources improve the learning experiences of our students?* If you can answer this question through storytelling, with the financial data to support the story, you will improve the level of support for your budget proposal within your community.

YOUR BUDGET PASSED—NOW WHAT?

Congratulations, you have successfully recommended your first budget to the school board—and they voted to accept it. Take a well-deserved moment to pat yourself on the back—this was no easy task. After your victory lap, you need to figure out what's next.

The truth is, the budget process really never stops. You must always find opportunities to share budget priorities, and then show the positive impact that funding the budget had on students when those priorities were funded. You must continue to tell the story to the staff, parents, and community about how the funding was used to impact children. You must continue to identify opportunities to share the needs, and the successes of funding certain priorities, to members of the school board and to other elected city or town officials that played a role in approving funding.

It is also important to communicate the successes of prioritizing school funding with the community. You should plan to provide updated communications on your budget successes throughout the year—always connecting to those stories that helped you to get the budget passed.

A word of caution: Many superintendents, school districts, principals, and school boards consider the work complete when budget approval is gained. It remains important, as the superintendent of schools, that you continue to monitor the progress of the budget priorities. Is implementation of those priorities meeting the anticipated expectations? If not, why not? Think about how you may need to intervene to ensure success.

One strategy that will support continued communication is the development and publication of an annual report for your district. The timing may differ, but a document like this would be helpful in ensuring that you communicate the success of the promises made during the development and approval process.

CONCLUSION

The budget development process is complicated, but is an important tool for school improvement. Too often this process is approached from a technical, "to-do" list perspective. Often missed is a real opportunity to leverage this process to improve the experiences of students. As you gain budgeting experience, you will gain fluency and credibility in the budget development process. As your credibility grows, you can propose increasingly unique approaches to improving the experience for students.

You may also be able to gain flexibility within the budget and propose multiyear pilots around positions or programs, with the understanding that if those approaches do not meet your anticipated outcomes, you will move on. This flexibility, and willingness to dismantle unsuccessful approaches and initiatives, will drive innovation, excitement, and improvement within your district. In the end, if successful, your management of the budget process will further support, and likely accelerate, school and district improvement to include worthwhile learning experiences for students in your district.

EXPERIENCES FROM THE FIELD

In my first year as superintendent in a two-thousand-student school district, I inherited a budget that had been reviewed, approved, and adopted by the school board. Due to some challenging fiscal times, the budget included the reduction of eight teaching positions.

In my early weeks and months, as I implemented my entry plan, I continued to hear from teachers and parents about the negative impact that eliminating eight teaching positions would have on student learning. I worked closely with the chief financial officer to better understand the process used to arrive at that level of reduction. While the process was fiscally sound, it did not center decision making on students.

As the fiscal year was underway, it felt like there was something we should do. I assembled a small group—me, the CFO, building principal, and our director of student services—to review the current budget and determine if there was any room to bring back any of the reduced positions. While we identified only two positions that we could return, the process employed was helpful in establishing a collaborative, problem-solving approach for the future. We were ultimately able to return all positions to the district the following year.

ADDITIONAL RESOURCES

Born, Clinton. *Making Sense of School Finance: A Practical State-by-State Approach.* Lanham, MD: Rowman & Littlefield, 2020.

Levenson, Nathan. *A Better Way to Budget: Building Support for Bold, Student-Centered Change in Public Schools.* Cambridge, MA: Harvard Education Press, 2015.

Levenson, Nathan. *Smarter Budgets, Smarter Schools: How to Survive and Thrive in Tight Times.* Cambridge, MA: Harvard Education Publishing Group, 2022.

Owings, William A., and Leslie S. Kaplan. *American Public School Finance.* London: Routledge, 2019.

Chapter 5

Relationship Building
Being Out and About

EXPERIENCES FROM THE FIELD

Imitation is the sincerest form of flattery. Many school administrators have borrowed, used, or replicated "best practices" from others they have learned from in educational leadership positions.

When I was a new teacher, a mentor teacher modeled the importance of interacting with students in the hallways and greeting students outside of the classroom before they entered for the class period. When I was a new principal, I learned from another experienced principal how to use a hallway desk to build stronger relationships with students and staff, be more visible, and be more efficient in my communications. And when I was a new superintendent, a veteran superintendent encouraged me to occasionally ride a school bus and/or eat lunch with students, and he also reminded me to routinely visit classrooms.

These ordinary everyday practices have become integral for me to build meaningful relationships, stay connected, and show I care about the people in the hallways, buses, cafeterias, and classrooms. They remain important parts of my practice to ensure that I stay connected to the student experience.

All superintendents should want to develop positive relationships with constituents, especially being new to the superintendency. Chapter 3 delved into the importance of nurturing relationships with school board members. Besides school board members, constituents can include students, parents, teachers and staff, administrators, community members, and other town leaders.

One way to convey your leadership is by sharing your vast experiences and educational know-how when it comes to guiding schools effectively. Another, and probably even more important, way to build relationships is to engage in daily positive interactions with people in your school district and community. Although this can oftentimes be somewhat random in nature, it is *essential*.

WE ALL WANT TO FEEL CONNECTED AND NEEDED

Perhaps you first went into education because you liked working with kids, enjoyed interacting with others, felt you would be a good role model, or maybe just wanted to avoid a desk job tucked away in a cubicle. We all want to feel needed, valued, and connected. Although as school superintendents we can all probably get more work done operating alone, it is not as fulfilling to work in isolation as it is to work with others. Connecting with people is what it's all about.

Besides being a school superintendent, perhaps you are also a parent, educator, community member, leader in your city or town that serves on a board, or even still a student in a master's or doctoral program. In those other roles, you are sure to gain appreciation and satisfaction when other people acknowledge or try to connect with you. Remember this as you interact with others as the superintendent of schools.

Reminding Us of Who We Are

People know who you are in your leadership position as school superintendent. Most people know that you are the superintendent when you are walking around in your school district. And if you ever forget you are the school superintendent at your job, you are reminded by the way people look at you, talk to you, or interact with you. So embrace these opportunities to lead education in your city or town.

Spending time in schools and classrooms should ground you and remind you of when you started as a classroom teacher or even further back when you were a student in the classroom yourself. As the superintendent, being in the classroom with teachers and students will likely become the best part of your days.

It's Not Always about You

It's really not so much about you as the superintendent as it is about the people in the town or city you are meeting, getting feedback from, and talking to. When interacting with others, it is important to think about how you might make people *feel*—how you make someone feel is probably more important than what you actually say.

What does your body language convey? Do you listen more than you talk? Do you lean forward and show interest with eye contact? In terms of conversing, do you sometimes interrupt others when they speak? Do you say "please" and "thank you" often enough? How you communicate is important to consider as you develop relationships with others in your school district.

Lifelong Learning

School superintendents have ample opportunities to lead. In addition to leading, it is important to show interest in learning from others in your school district. Superintendents should show others in their school district(s) that they are willing to learn from their peers and other employees—teachers, paraprofessionals, custodians, and secretaries. Superintendents should make efforts to sign up for and show up at some internal professional development sessions. Then they should stay for the duration of these workshops and learn as an active participant in the school or district session.

Learning outside of the district is equally important. Superintendents need to stay current in educational topics and best practices by attending conferences and workshops, and by reading professional publications and articles. Effective superintendents will glean information received, relate relevant topics to their work as the district leader, and then adapt what they learned by connecting it to district work and sharing it with their leadership teams, teachers, and staff.

GETTING OUT OF YOUR OFFICE

Too many superintendents spend much of their time in their offices or in the comfortable company of their central office administrative staff. It is important to avoid the bad habit of spending too much time in the office. Superintendents who develop bad habits, and who are not visible, can be perceived as ineffective or disconnected.

Being out and about in the different schools is the best way to experience the real culture of each school, collect anecdotal data, and see things firsthand as the district superintendent. Being seen and heard in person helps others to see who you are, hear what you are about, and know that you care.

Conduct School Visits

It is important to spend time in schools—this is where you will see things, hear things, and experience things in an unfiltered way. Depending on the size of your school district, you could try to conduct visits to individual schools weekly, biweekly, monthly, bimonthly, or quarterly. Ideally, you would schedule routine meetings with the principal to frame the visit, and then after facilitating that meeting with the principal, you would walk alongside the principal through classrooms, hallways, and other high-traffic areas such as the cafeteria. You could even plan to have lunch with a small group of students from the school to hear about their school experiences.

In speaking about working to develop a positive school and district culture, Joe Sanfelippo and Tony Sinanis state, "Because a school's culture extends to all of its stakeholders, effective interactions are the single most important non-negotiable in creating flourishing schools."[1] Interacting with people is collaborative, and respectful collaboration breeds trust. Leaders who spend time appreciating the people in the trenches who are doing the most important work with the students are typically respected and gain trust more readily from their staff.

School visits are important. These visits allow you to experience the climate and culture of a building, assess a principal's effectiveness, and make continued connections with people within each building. Undoubtedly, the best part of your day will be spent interacting informally with students, staff, teachers, and principals.

In engaging in this supervision by walking around, many superintendents have had opportunities to observe people doing commendable things, laugh with people, console people, and bond with people. How wonderful it is when people connect with the superintendent for who they are as a person and not just who they are as superintendent.

Attend Sporting Events

Being present for your teams is a wonderful way to support your student-athletes and coaches. Athletic matches can be the among the most well-attended events that your schools host. One strategy is to have your administrative assistant schedule you to attend at least one home sporting event, game, match, or meet for each team sport season. When there, cheer on your home teams.

Be engaged. Ask about and encourage the students on the teams. Talk to and get to know the coaches (without disrupting them from coaching the games). If you have inclusive "unified" sports teams, be sure to include these in the home sporting events you attend. Also think about attending the playoffs if any of your teams do well in their postseason runs.

Show Up to Various Extracurricular Events

Aside from sporting events, it is important to support and encourage students and staff who participate in various clubs, the arts, or extracurricular activities. Superintendents who attend events and activities such as drama productions, choral or band concerts, GSA (gender and sexuality alliance) club meetings, and some other after-school clubs such as debate or chess club are seen as supportive, inclusive, and interested in student and staff interests. It is crucial for a school superintendent to learn about students and staff who are passionate about certain interests and topics.

Attend City or Town Meetings or Town-Wide Events

It pays to show interest and be invested in city or town business. In addition to an annual meeting where a superintendent may need to present their school department budget or talk about capital improvement needs to the city or town leaders, a superintendent should attend some other city or town meetings to express interest in local business. This is particularly important if there are items being discussed that may impact the schools or focus on school-aged children. These meetings or events can also be opportunities for superintendents to advocate for school improvements that other constituents may be interested in or able to help with.

A superintendent can and should be able to attend a local board of health meeting, capital improvement committee meeting, or city council or select board meeting. If a school building project is getting started, the superintendent might also end up at a zoning board meeting or conservation committee meeting.

Superintendents should also attend some school building committee meetings once a new school is being built, or an older school is getting accelerated repairs, or some city or town fields that students use are being renovated. If you can't attend some of these meetings as the superintendent, try to watch the meeting(s) later if televised, or read the meeting minutes.

Some Other Things You Can Do to Be Visible and Connected

In addition to some of the things already mentioned in this chapter, there are other simple things you can do as the superintendent to be visible and connected.

Ride the School Bus

Take some time each year to ride a school bus from an identified student's home bus stop. Be sure to get permission from the student's parent or guardian and also get clearance from the bus company and bus driver first. Another benefit is that you experience what students experience firsthand, helping you to see opportunities for improvement that might exist.

Use a Hallway Desk

Use a desk located in the hallway at each school in the district for at least a few days. This helps people in the schools know who you are as the superintendent. Students will ask who you are. The hallway desk not only makes it easier to chat with students, but also to engage in informal conversations with custodians, teachers, principals, and other staff.

One time a high school student approached me and asked, "Are you the guy who I should talk to about getting rid of finals?" This made me smile, as apparently a teacher told him to ask me because I was "the guy over there [at my hallway desk] in charge." I then replied, "No, that's your high school principal!"

Write Personalized, Handwritten Thank-You Notes

Aside from writing notes of condolence for something like a death in the family, or a congratulatory note for something like earning a master's degree, it is important to show appreciation and recognize the exceptional work or accomplishments of those who work in your school district. If possible, mail the thank-you note to the person's home address. You may be surprised by the amount of positive feedback that you receive for this easy act. You will also stay close to the many individual stories of success that happen every day in your district.

The thank-you note could acknowledge the recipient for a positive interaction you witnessed them have with a student. Or the note could simply say that you enjoyed the conversation you had recently with them. Regardless of the reason, it's the thoughtful gesture that counts.

CONVEYING YOUR SENSE OF PURPOSE

Being visible is a relatively easy goal to achieve. It is important to remember that being visible is not about just being visible. During these times you will have opportunities to interact with many people in your community. It is important to think about, and try to convey, your sense of purpose.

What is your *why*? What do you do, or don't do, with your time? What do you stand for and believe in, or don't believe in, based on what you say? What are you trying to accomplish, or trying to avoid, based on what you do? Who do you value, or who do you not value, based on what you say and whom you spend your time with?

Having a sense of purpose means you want to accomplish meaningful things as part of your work as superintendent. You need to believe that what you do each day can have a positive impact on others, which will in turn contribute to making the school district better. Even when faced with setbacks, which every superintendent will experience, you need to move forward with positive intent and direction.

If you don't convey any sense of purpose, it is a problem. Others will perceive your sense of purpose for you and likely make assumptions about your intentions and values based on whom you spend your time with . . . or don't spend time with; what you do . . . or don't do, and what you say . . . or don't say.

BUILDING POSITIVE PERSONAL RELATIONSHIPS WITH CONSTITUENTS

Relationship building is tantamount to the success and longevity of a superintendent. Demonstrating good people skills means you can relate to others, be a good listener, ask relevant questions, show humor, and act in a genuine way. Relationships can be built with good communication, which can be face-to-face, on the phone, or via email correspondence. Below are some ways you can build positive relationships with stakeholders and constituents in your school community.

Host Brief Meetings with Everyone You Can Think Of

Chapter 3 delves into the importance of meeting regularly with individual current school board members. Besides current board members, there are so many other constituents in your school district's city or town for you to meet and get to know. From the mayor or town manager to elected officials to partners in emergency services, your relationships with these people will matter . . . *a lot*.

You will learn so much, past and present, from these new people you talk to. You will also have a group of people that you can turn to in times of challenge or adversity. These relationships matter when you are dealing with an emergency and need to talk with the police chief directly, for example.

Especially when you get started as a new superintendent, you should schedule brief thirty-minute meetings with as many constituents as you can think of. Some people you may want to meet with are all administrators, individual school PTO (parent-teacher organization) presidents, the police chief, the fire chief, city or town council members, the mayor or town administrator, high school student-leaders, school-based curriculum leaders, certain teachers with a historical context of the school district, past school board members, and those community members who carry sway but do not have an official title or affiliation. You may also consider finding time to connect with other groups in your community and visit the senior center, local Realtors, and service clubs (e.g., Lions, Rotary, Kiwanis) in your community.

Think of a few basic questions to ask these people in your introductory meetings. For example, you can plan to conduct an informal SWOT (strengths, weaknesses, opportunities, threats) analysis by asking the following questions in your thirty-minute meetings:

- What has gone well (i.e., strengths)?
- What does the school district need to work on (i.e., weaknesses)?
- Where do you see untapped potential in the district (i.e., opportunities)?
- Are there any current challenges (i.e., threats) to our success?

These meetings will essentially help you get to know a lot of key players in a relatively short amount of time. You will also learn a wealth of information to help you move the district forward into the future.

Get Engaged in Some Work of the Community You Serve

Being invested and interested in some of the work in the community you serve is very important. Even if the superintendent does not live in the city or town in which they serve as the superintendent, it is important for the school district's leader to take some interest and participate in certain events when given the opportunity.

If there is an annual event celebrated in the city or town, the superintendent can attend and perhaps volunteer at this event in some capacity. If there is a carwash fundraiser for a sports team that happens to be taking place when the superintendent is in the area, the school superintendent should swing by and get their car washed. If there is a local food pantry collecting canned goods, the superintendent can contribute. And if there is a fall cleanup day happening, perhaps the superintendent can rake some leaves for an hour or two with the other volunteers.

Serve on School Building Committees

If given the opportunity, a superintendent would undoubtedly be a valuable member of a school building committee or town committee working to upgrade school district facilities or fields. Some cities or towns may have charter rules or policies that prohibit a superintendent from serving on a building committee if they do not reside in that city or town. Even if the superintendent does not live in the city or town they work in, and they cannot be an official building committee member, superintendents can still attend these public meetings and perhaps serve as an "ad hoc" member of these committees.

Attending building committee meetings can often lead to interactions with new people who live in the school district and support the schools. These interactions can lead to fruitful conversations and new partnerships that may bring more credibility and, ultimately, some welcomed goodwill to the school system. School superintendents who express not just support, but also the dedication to see a building project through, will be respected.

Work with Local Benevolent Groups

Being superintendent will expose you to many well-meaning groups and organizations. Some organizations may contact you and some others may not; it is up to you to determine which groups you want to become involved with, and how much time to spend. It is vital to take time to support a local food pantry, recycling or sustainability committee, Boys & Girls Club, youth sports organization, or perhaps even a parent-owned restaurant or retail establishment.

Return an email from a community member who reaches out to you as the superintendent for acknowledgment or support. Look around your house and make that personal donation to the food pantry. Support one of your elementary school's PTOs by purchasing a ticket to one of their sponsored events. Attend an event hosted by your Special Education Parent Advisory Council or booster clubs. Have conversations with leaders of these organizations to let them know you sincerely appreciate, value, and support their volunteerism.

CONCLUSION

In the end, relationship building may be more important than anything else a superintendent does with their time. To build relationships, you need to spend considerable time with the people doing the most important work with your students. When striving to build relationships integral to the success of your students, remember to listen more than you talk, learn as much as (or more than) you lead, show up, and get engaged in the work of the community you serve.

EXPERIENCES FROM THE FIELD

As a new superintendent, at first I felt like everything was about me. I was excited to have people get to know me as a leader and as a person . . . but I was thinking it was more about them knowing me than me knowing them as individuals. After the summer concluded and I was able to spend considerable time in classrooms, I realized the superintendency was more about the teachers, students, families, and principals than myself. I learned that the superintendent role was ultimately more to serve as lead advocate than as the center of attention. Spending time in schools, classrooms, and at events reminded me of this role to appreciate and serve others.

As superintendent of schools, you need to know your "why." Your efforts should be focused on meeting the needs of the students and the people you serve. Being a district superintendent calls on you to focus on relationship building. Your success will come only after you spend time getting to know people in your school district, build positive relationships, and embed yourself in the community.

ADDITIONAL RESOURCES

Blad, E. "Tips for Building Strong Principal-Superintendent Relationships." *Education Week*, March 24, 2022. https://www.edweek.org/leadership/tips-for-building-strong-principal-superintendent-relationships/2022/03.

Hackett, Julie L. *Building Relationships Yielding Results: How Superintendents Can Work with School Boards to Create Productive Teams*. Cambridge, MA: Harvard Education Press, 2015.

Leverett, L. "Engaging the Public: A Superintendent's View." Edutopia, September 1, 2000. https://www.edutopia.org/engaging-public-superintendents-view.

Chapter 6

The Joys of Personnel Management

From Recruitment to Retirement

EXPERIENCES FROM THE FIELD

It was my first year as superintendent and, following the winter sports season, I learned about multiple concerns that were raised about a coach. The athletic director and principal both recommended that we not renew the coach's employment. The coach had been working for the district for nine seasons and had brought our high school team to two league championships. The principal met with the coach to notify him that he would not be returning as coach the following year.

The coach took to social media to share this news and also shared how unfair he thought it was. Immediately we started to receive a significant number of email messages from community members extolling the virtues of the coach and demanding reconsideration of the decision. At the next school board meeting, we had nearly one hundred attendees, all to support the coach. This situation proved to be incredibly challenging and persisted for weeks. To this day, that was one of the most contentious school committee meetings I attended.

Since then I have never underestimated the potential impact of hiring/ termination decisions. While I would make the same decision today, that experience helped me understand how to better prepare for and handle a situation like this.

KEY COMPONENTS OF MANAGING PERSONNEL

As a school superintendent you will find that you play a major role in all aspects of personnel policy, practices, and decisions. Regardless of the structure of your school district, you will be involved in personnel matters, and you should *want* to be involved. As you begin your superintendency, you will see that personnel matters will take up a substantial amount of your time at work—after all, it is the individuals who work in your school district who will determine whether you are providing the very best possible education for all of your students.

Like many of the major responsibilities of the school superintendent, you will need to keep in close contact with your human resources department—if you are lucky enough to have one. This will foster your understanding of staffing challenges and existing opportunities. Your partnership with the human resources department will support your decision making so that your workforce is the most talented it can be to support student learning. Your ongoing monitoring of and partnership with personnel management will also enable hiring processes to align with both your core values and those of the district.

As you conceptualize your work in this area, it may be helpful to put the major components of personnel management into categories. By doing so, you will be able to review and evaluate the practices within each area of your school district. This approach will also allow you to assess the relative strengths (or weaknesses) in each area so that you can make changes as necessary. Categories to be reviewed include the following:

- Recruitment
- Interview and hiring procedures
- Onboarding new employees
- Assessing and supporting the district and school culture
- Demonstrating care
- Managing difficult personnel

Recruitment

The teacher shortage is real. While districts have felt challenges of hiring teachers—particularly in math and science—for some time the COVID-19 pandemic has seemed to further impact the number of available candidates for teaching as well as for administrative positions. Many local, state, and federal agencies are now engaged in working to improve the pipeline of teacher candidates to schools.[1]

While focusing on the work of improving the pipeline of educators is exciting, it is not likely to bear fruit for some time. As a result, districts must develop plans to increase interaction with qualified candidates who will enhance the core values of the district.

The impact of the teacher shortage, combined with the impact of the pandemic, has been significant. Teacher burnout following the more than two years of managing the pandemic has led to many experienced teachers either leaving the profession or looking for positions in new districts. While in the past a very experienced teacher may not have been able to land a new position—largely due to the cost of hiring someone with a high level of experience—the rules have shifted and these individuals have been able to take advantage of more mobility and need within the profession.

It remains to be seen whether these current circumstances will persist. It is also unknown whether this will ultimately be a good shift for the profession. What is clear is that, as superintendent, you will need to plan for how your district will react and respond to this circumstance. If you rely on traditional practices to recruit staff, you may find that you have difficulty recruiting top talent to your district. After examining the practices in your district, determine whether any of the following will support elevating the reputation of your school district to assist in recruiting:

- Branding and marketing of your district
- Participating in job fairs
- Forging formal partnerships with colleges/universities
- Offering unique benefits

Branding and Marketing of Your District

Given the teacher and staffing shortage we are facing, districts need to step up their profile among potential candidates. While some parts of the country have been dealing with competition to find teachers between districts, the current-day circumstances have thrust more districts into this reality. In many areas, we have been able to rely on the imbalance of more candidates than available positions. As this balance has changed, we must consider ways to help our districts stand out from others. You and your team must develop a plan to sell your district to prospective teachers and other staff.

It is likely that no one in your school district will have the background to support the development of a marketing campaign to raise the district's profile. After all, we are in the business of education, not marketing. This is an area where identifying and partnering with a consultant would be helpful. The right consultant will help you develop a recruitment video, ensure your "brand" is consistent across platforms, outline a plan to increase your social media presence, and connect the district with new methods of reaching potential employees.

These strategies, when well executed, will help to raise the profile of your school district. A direct result should be that more qualified candidates, who may not have even known about your district, apply for open positions.

Participating in Job Fairs

Job fairs and hiring fairs have been used for a long time in recruitment efforts. In particular, large districts use job fairs and hiring fairs as a primary strategy to recruit candidates. Some larger school districts will employ a team of individuals to travel the country and engage in recruitment through job fairs.

While some districts have embraced this approach, many have sat by waiting for candidates to come to them. In many cases this approach worked. Again, with the shrinking candidate pool, you should carefully consider your district's participation in a wide range of job fairs. Depending on the focus of the job fair, you will be able to gain access to candidates who may not have ever considered your district. It will also allow you to continue to promote your district, and its unique attributes, to a wider audience.

Forging Formal Partnerships with Colleges/Universities

Another supportive recruitment effort is to develop formal and long-term partnerships with colleges and universities. A partnership with a college or university, particularly one with a teacher education program, will improve your access to new graduates. For many school districts the extent of the partnership between a college or university and the school district is to host a few student-teachers annually. There are many more opportunities to leverage a partnership with a college or university to support efforts to recruit teachers to your school district.

Other opportunities include formalizing fellow or intern programs for other professionals within your district (e.g., school psychologists, adjustment counselors). A relationship of this nature could support ongoing access to hard-to-find candidates. In this type of relationship, your district may pay the college to have a fellow join your staff for a year. The fellow or intern can then benefit because part or all of their education costs may be covered through this approach.

A school district might launch a partnership with a college or university to include graduate programs developed and supported by the district. Because some states require teachers to obtain their master's degree to continue to be licensed, this type of partnership may be particularly attractive. In this approach, the employee can access a low- or no-cost graduate program to support their continued—and required—professional growth and credentialing.

Further, with a partnership of this type, a district may be able to collaborate in the development of this program so that it aligns with the district's core values, mission, and major initiatives. A district-developed and -supported program would also provide additional opportunities for experienced staff. These staff members may be given the opportunity to teach as an adjunct professor within the program or engage in other professional development activities that are highly contextualized to the aims of the district.

Another potential benefit of a district-developed and -supported program is cost. Cost-wise, the district may benefit in a few ways. As part of the recruitment strategy, a district-developed program may be offered at a reduced cost to participants. In addition, depending on the district's benefit to teachers related to tuition reimbursement, the district may find that the costs of tuition reimbursement is less for employees who participate in this jointly developed graduate program.

Finally, another potential area of partnership is research. A research partnership with a university could provide many benefits to the district and to the larger field of education. Being open to offering your district as a place where you embrace and conduct educational research could become another draw for interested candidates. In addition, allowing experienced teachers to develop and conduct their own research, under the guidance of the university, could support continued engagement of more experienced teachers in the profession.

Offering Unique Benefits

While salary may also be the primary driver of decision making around employment decisions, other factors also matter. For example, it will likely matter to potential candidates if your district provides any unique benefits that will help sell your district.

We have all heard of the sometimes luxurious benefits that employees of big technology companies are offered. You should identify and highlight the unique employment benefits of your district. While many candidates will look at tangible benefits like salary to inform their decisions, other benefits could support a candidate choosing your district over another, even if that other district pays more in terms of salary. Some of the benefits that districts have offered employees include the following:

- Sign-on bonuses
- Research partnerships with universities (previously mentioned)
- Ability to elect to have their children attend your district
- Employee daycare

- Discounted or free before-school and after-school programming for their children
- Student loan repayment or support
- Support with affordable housing
- Employee wellness and discount programs
- Sabbatical option following a specified number of years of experience

It is likely that your new district has some unique characteristics. You need to find them and highlight them to potential candidates. You might find that it is one of these unique benefits that result in your ideal candidate saying "yes."

Interview and Hiring Procedures

Your recruitment efforts, if effective, should lead to a large pool of candidates from which you and your team can choose. With successful strategies around recruitment, you can turn your attention to interviewing and hiring procedures.

Interviewing and hiring practices in schools and districts are essential to create an excellent match between a candidate and a school. It is important that you clearly articulate your values around interviewing and hiring practices. Again, if you are fortunate enough to have a human resources department, a briefing from the individual who manages that department will support your understanding of whether the practices align with your core values.

Interviewing Practices

Depending on local conditions and traditions, interviewing may be conducted through a centralized process, or an individual school building. In either circumstance, you must insist on consistency of practices. You must decide on the requirements that will guide the process as it is developed. Once determined, your district leadership team must adhere to those practices in nearly all circumstances, while there may be some exceptions. Some considerations include the following:

- Minimum number of rounds of the interview process
- Collaborative interview committees
- Model lessons for teachers
- Reference checks

Interview Rounds

Working with an ideal timeline, how many interview rounds will you require of your hiring manager before making a final decision on a candidate?

For example, you might adopt a practice where all applicants are screened through your human resources department via a ten-minute phone interview. You might decide that you will include a requirement that all candidates add a statement of educational philosophy.

The goal of this approach as a starting point is to make each applicant aware of the details of the position that they applied for, to alert them to any incomplete areas of their submitted materials, and to share with them the timeline of the first round of interviews.

The first round of interviews should include an interview committee. It is important that members of the interview committee understand their specific role in the committee. Is the committee's purpose to identify a finalist candidate, or multiple candidates that they will send forward to the next round? Is the interview committee a decision-making or advisory body? In either case, the interview committee should be made up of broad representatives from the school with the open position.

Where possible, the interview committee should include teachers of similar grade or content area to the candidate being interviewed, building-level administrators, and students. The optimal goal of this group is to conduct an interview and identify multiple candidates to move forward as finalists.

Once the interview committee has completed its process and finalists have been identified, finalist candidates can be contacted to come back to perform a model lesson. Ideally this lesson will be the same grade or subject area for which the candidate is interviewing. The model lesson will provide the hiring manager with an opportunity to see the candidate in action, with a focus on their teaching skill.

Following the model lesson, there should be an opportunity for the hiring manager to meet with the candidate and debrief the lesson experience. This will provide the hiring manager with another perspective on the candidate—specifically, whether the candidate is a teacher who reflects on their practices and is able to effectively identify opportunities for improvement.

Following the conclusion of the interview rounds and the model lessons, the principal or other hiring manager (e.g., department head) may feel ready to make a decision. The final step in the process is to conduct reference checks. There are some common pitfalls with reference checks.

First, many hiring managers either ignore the obligation to complete them or they conduct them as a perfunctory activity. Second, many hiring managers will only call the references the candidate has included in their application materials. While those individuals will help you acquire a better understanding of the candidate, they are self-selected. As part of your requirements, you might insist that your hiring managers contact colleagues and supervisors of candidates who are not listed in the application materials. More specifically, references who are the *current direct supervisor* of the finalist candidate should be contacted.

Onboarding New Employees

After all of this, the district is ready to make the job offer. You must decide how the offer will be made. This is important and will speak volumes about the values of your district around caring for and supporting employees. Will you have a mini-celebration for each candidate offered a position? Will every candidate attend an orientation prior to starting a position within your district? Whatever you decide, keep in mind that these early experiences of a new employee will have an impact on their impression of the district. The approach you choose will help to reinforce the adult culture you are trying to develop.

Assessing and Supporting the District and School Culture

Prior to the COVID-19 pandemic, working in education was difficult. Being a teacher is a calling that requires a high degree of skill and an incredible emotional investment. As mentioned earlier, anyone working in education was deeply impacted by the pandemic. The deep worry about students, while also worrying about the safety and security of our own families, added layers of complexity to this already difficult work. As we have begun to recover from the pandemic, or at least normalize the continuing impact of the pandemic, there has been another challenge. The political climate has shifted and, in many cases, put educators at the center of some vitriol and negativity.

What has always been consistent is that, as school superintendent, you need to understand your district's culture and climate. Pinning down where your district and individual schools are regarding the culture and climate can be difficult. There are many ways that you might approach gaining an improved understanding of the climate within your school district. Below are a few ideas:

- Faculty and staff advisory committees: This structure includes holding regular meetings with faculty and staff who provide you with feedback and information on the current climate of the district and share ideas about actions you might take to improve the climate.
- Informal school visits: You may visit schools for events or for meetings, but this approach encourages you to get out of your office and be available and accessible to faculty and staff. You could begin by putting a planned informal visit on your calendar each week. Plan on being

present in the schools, without an agenda, to connect with faculty and staff, and carefully listen to their feedback and input.
- Exit interviews: A helpful approach to learn more about culture and climate is to verify that someone is conducting exit interviews of employees who are leaving the district. The exit interview should include questions that probe the employee's experiences and allow them to share what the school or school district could do better to support its staff. The results of exit interviews should be regularly reviewed and shared with the district leadership team.
- Formal surveys: There are a number of companies that provide an electronic and anonymous staff climate survey for school districts. Surveys used over time will allow you to follow trends to see if the district's efforts to improve the culture and climate are paying off. Depending on the survey instrument you choose, you may also gain an understanding of how your district compares to other similar districts.

Demonstrating Care

You are now the superintendent of a school district with hundreds or thousands of employees. The sheer scale of the individuals that work for your district may be daunting, but it remains important that you do what you can to let all employees know that they are valued and seen. Your modeled leadership in this area will be a clear signal to your leadership team about the importance of caring for your staff—and showing that you care. This will result in an important ripple effect across your district.

You might be thinking that your district is too large to do this well. Or that you will not be able to develop a system you can keep up over time. There are some systematic approaches that you can implement to show care, some of which were described above as ways to assess school culture and climate. Some other ideas include the following:

- Informal school visits: As already mentioned, informal school visits will allow you to assess the culture and climate of schools. You can also use this same model to engage casually with faculty and staff, ask them about their work, and identify opportunities where you can provide support.
- Send personal notes to recognize events: The staff will experience many highlights in their careers and personal lives. They will also suffer sadness and loss. In both cases, consider sending a personal note or card to recognize the birth of a child, or the achievement of a master's degree. Send sympathy cards when a staff member experiences loss, or a get-well card if someone is dealing with a significant health issue. It will

be important that you work with your assistant to systematize a process to make you consistently send out notes.
- The coffee cart: Some colleagues have used a coffee cart to take a moment to share thanks and appreciation to faculty and staff, especially during those most challenging times of the school year. In this approach, you and other district or school leaders will push a "coffee cart" around the school and offer faculty and staff refreshment. Staff will appreciate the refreshment in the midst of their busy day. They will also appreciate that you have taken the time to do this yourself. Another benefit is you are able to engage briefly with individual employees of your district.
- Make a day special: As school superintendent you have the authority to disrupt the norm. Use that authority as a way to lift up your staff. You might arrange to provide breakfast or lunch for everyone, have cookies sent to a faculty meeting, or send staff a small gift as a token of appreciation. Whatever it is, think about finding the opportunity to make the day special for faculty and staff.
- Help out: Another opportunity is to go back to your roots and help out in buildings. You might schedule regular opportunities to substitute-teach in buildings. We certainly saw more of this take place as a matter of need during the staffing challenges of the pandemic. You might also decide to help out at morning arrival, afternoon dismissal, and lunch or recess duty. All of these approaches will put you in contact in informal settings that allow you to more easily share your appreciation of their work.
- Use technology: There are many platforms that support culture building within professional communities. These platforms rely on amplifying the voices of all staff to publicly thank colleagues. When connected to your district's core values, this can be a powerful approach. These platforms may also use a token economy to award recognition and allow staff to turn in their rewards for tangible items. This idea is very common in the private sector.

Sharing your appreciation and care for faculty and staff is important. In doing so, you will model how you would like your district leadership team to engage and interact with their faculty and staff as well. The goal, of course, is to convey to your staff that you care about them and their work. In the end, you need to find a system and approach that is most comfortable for you and best aligns with your personality.

Managing Difficult Personnel

Staff issues for a superintendent could be compared to student issues that a principal manages. As superintendents, we may often also think like a principal. For example, should you provide assistance or discipline? Should you suspend an employee or just write a letter of expectations? Should you signal a message of disappointment or show empathy?

As a superintendent, there can be a balance between coaching and reprimanding. When working with a principal, should you coach the principal to be more lenient or strict? Like everything else, it depends on the situation at hand.

It is important to keep in mind that schools and districts are complicated organizations. Depending on your context, you could have more than a dozen types of employee groups. Embedded within the groups could be multiple collectively bargained agreements (union contracts) that you must take into consideration prior to any employee action. To make matters even more complex, expectations and processes that you are required to follow may not be aligned between the various employee groups. Your first obligation is to understand the conditions specific to your district context.

An effective means of gaining initial insight into a specific context is to start by reading all of the employee agreements. This is another area where a human resources department could be helpful. Whether union contracts or individual agreements, these documents will provide you with some follow-up questions that you will ask the human resources department. Following your review of relevant documents, you will want to more clearly understand how the agreements are put into practice.

After you have been able to gain a broad understanding of contracts and employee types, you need to continue to review relevant documents, especially as situations arise that are already addressed in the collectively bargained contracts. You should work with your human resources staff to gain access to investigations related to employees. You will also want to spend some time with the district's legal counsel that has worked with and supported the district around employee issues.

The district's legal counsel is also a good place to learn more. When speaking to legal counsel, you should seek information about the circumstances when the district has called to ask for an opinion in the past. Were there any areas that regularly resulted in the district calling legal counsel? While it is unlikely that you will make any changes initially as you learn more about past practices of the district regarding personnel decisions, understanding the historical vulnerabilities that the district has experienced will allow you to begin to form potential interventions to support improvement.

Any organization with hundreds or thousands of employees will inevitably find itself dealing with difficult employee challenges such as complaints, grievances to the contracts, or general poor behavior and bad decision making of employees. It is impossible to work through the wide range of scenarios that you might encounter. When you are faced with these situations, you should answer the following questions before acting:

- Has a situation similar to this occurred before? If so, what was the process and outcome?
- Is there a concern of the violation of law? If so, consult your legal counsel.
- Does the situation require an investigation? If so, who will conduct the investigation? And what framework will be considered when conducting the investigation? Also, contact legal counsel as needed.
- Does the situation violate established district core values, or your core values?
- What due process processes are you required to follow to manage the situation?

Depending on your path to the school superintendency, this may be a relatively new area of responsibility. As previously mentioned, a typical school district has multiple employee groups that may require different handling techniques to ensure compliance with internal procedures and external requirements.

It is advisable to plan to spend more time connecting with the district's legal counsel during your first year so that you obtain the guidance necessary to make decisions that are fair, just, and in compliance with requirements. In addition, you should have a conversation with your school board chair about your approach to access legal counsel. If you don't, the optics of increased legal fees may be misconstrued as an area of weakness rather than a proactive, learning stance you are taking.

YOU'RE AN EMPLOYEE, TOO

As you consider how you will manage the employees within your organization, it is important to remember that you are an employee too. As you make adjustments to practices and policies for employees, you must consider how they will, and should, impact you. As an employee, like any other, it will be important not to take special advantage of your position. Your modeling of behavior around these changes will be important.

One area in which you should exercise some latitude is your contract. As a new superintendent, depending on rules in your state, you may have received a contract of three years or less. As you successfully complete the first year of your contract, you have established yourself as a leader who can get the important work done. Well done!

Now is the time to talk with your school board about extending your contract. The purpose of this discussion is not about improving your salary and benefits, although that would be great, but instead to signal to the school board and community your deep commitment to the work within your district. The overriding goal is to take the time needed in the role to enact any required changes and to make improvements for students.

CONCLUSION

Personnel management is complicated and ever-changing. As the district's leader, your behaviors in this area will reverberate across the district and send messages to every staff member. The message you want to send must be thought out and acted on in your daily interactions as you manage this complexity. In the end, it is your responsibility to ensure that each interaction is respectful and shows care for others. This will often require that you model what you expect of others and also take the high ground when dealing with personnel issues—these are things that great leaders do.

EXPERIENCES FROM THE FIELD

As an experienced superintendent I was fortunate to serve in a community that had a high level of regard for the importance of public education. The support of the community was often very visible during the budget development process, where community members demanded growth and improvement in our schools.

More recently, with the economic winds shifting, I found myself for the first time in a situation where we had to make significant reductions to balance a budget. This was a new experience for me, as well as the school committee. With personnel costs consuming the lion's share of the budget, it was clear that some difficult decisions would have to be made. After working closely with the leadership team, we identified necessary reductions.

The conversations with impacted employees that followed were some of the most difficult conversations I have had. It was important to me to be the one who shared the news and explain why we were in that situation. At that moment, as a leader, I thought it was the right thing to do.

ADDITIONAL RESOURCES

Coyle, Daniel. *The Culture Code: The Secrets of Highly Successful Groups*. New York: Random House, 2018.

Darfler-Sweeney, Patrick. *The Superintendent's Rulebook: A Guide to District-Level Leadership*. London: Taylor & Francis, 2018.

Hannaway, Jane, and Andrew J. Rotherham. *Collective Bargaining in Education: Negotiating Change in Today's Schools*. Cambridge, MA: Harvard Education Press, 2006.

Rebore, Ronald W. *The Essentials of Human Resources Administration in Education*. Munich: Pearson, 2012.

Chapter 7

Hear Ye, Hear Ye!
Effective Communication Strategies

EXPERIENCES FROM THE FIELD

I recall a situation where we began reviewing the math curriculum materials we were using at the elementary level. The program we had been using was just not meeting our needs and it was time for a change. We went through a very intentional process that included establishing a committee of elementary teachers, principals, and the assistant superintendent to begin to review available products that might better meet our needs.

This group met for nearly a year before making a recommendation to purchase new curriculum materials. The team was very excited and believed that these new materials would result in an improvement of the experience for kids.

During the budget process we shared with the school committee the needs we identified for the upcoming school year, including the need to purchase these new math curriculum materials. To my great surprise, and embarrassment, this was the first time that the school committee had heard about this team and the recommendation that they were making—even though the team had been meeting for nearly a year. While the school committee ultimately accepted the recommendation, this did not go well.

From that point on, whenever there is a major initiative of the district, we also develop a communications plan to ensure that we are sharing updates and progress in a regular and transparent way. That way no one is surprised when you get to the point of final approval.

EFFECTIVE COMMUNICATION

An important prerequisite for moving into the role of the superintendent is excellent communication. There is almost no doubt that you have already checked that box—after all, you were able to make it through the search process and get appointed as the superintendent. Now that you are in the role, effectively communicating with an expanded number of constituent groups is your responsibility.

To add complexity to this challenge, you must balance the requirement to communicate many pieces of information—often complex ideas or initiatives—to many groups, each with a slightly different perspective on the information or initiative.

This chapter explores many of the complicated practices and strategies related to communicating effectively. Included is information related to communication challenges, using social media, establishing a cadence, and thinking about different approaches to deal with communication around times of crisis.

Through the implementation of specific strategies, you will communicate in a way that is highly relevant, effective, and will help you build credibility within your community. Whether you have the benefit of a communications director or not, the development of a reliable and deliberate communication strategy will support school improvement within your district.

COMMUNICATION CHALLENGES

It is likely that during your career you have been surprised, disappointed, or dismayed by the fact that someone did not understand your very clear communication about an important issue or topic. You worked so hard to share a clear, succinct, and understandable message that explained, in painstaking detail, what you wanted to convey. The single biggest problem in communication is the illusion that it has taken place, an utterance credited to George Bernard Shaw. George was right.

Most of us believe that once we have given that speech, sent that email, or facilitated that meeting, the receiver has clearly understood the message. More often than not, however, this is not the case. One of the biggest oversights in our communication is that we believe that it is completed when or just after the communication takes place.

So what happened? Why did your perfectly crafted communication fail to provide the clarity you anticipated? Effectively communicating a simple idea or concept, in and of itself, is a challenge. Once you add the complexity of the concept, and pair that with increasingly complicated language that is specific to the education space, this process becomes arduous. And if the communication also includes information about a coming change in a program or approach, or a new initiative, the communication becomes even more difficult.

The challenge is significant, and deciding to give up and not attempt to communicate these important pieces of information is not an option—this situation calls for a reset. You need to rethink your communication strategies and put in place systems and processes that will improve your success. It is important to remember that effective communication cannot be effectively delivered in a singular act (e.g., speech, email, meeting), unless it is a very simplistic item. Instead, *consider communication as a series of acts that should be repeated and reinforced.*

The concept of communication requiring an ongoing series of events is not new. Research has demonstrated that successfully communicating a message is not a singular event. Instead, effectively communicating a message requires repeated events to communicate that message. Marketing research has studied this concept extensively and landed on a rule of seven events being necessary to most likely create awareness for the consumer.[1] While we are talking about school district stakeholders, not potential customers, the research may be helpful as we contemplate a communications plan.

To reflect on and consider changes to your communication strategy, you must first admit that communication is complicated and you are not as good at it as you believe. Adhering to this growth mindset will open you up to the idea that with examination and work, you can improve. In addition, this changed perspective will allow you to consider implementing a specific system and process that helps you improve communication.

A clear communication strategy that is articulated, understood, and followed by other members of your leadership team will create cross-team accountability so that important messages are being shared, early and often, to all of the connected stakeholders. Additionally, the implementation of a system will create some automaticity among you and your team around communication strategies that you have seen are more effective.

A typical complaint from a school community is that communication from the school is overburdened with "eduspeak" and is often too difficult to understand or follow. A key tenet of a communication strategy must include norms around structure and language that will be used. For example, you must avoid educational jargon and limit the use of acronyms. Succinct and simple systems of communication will allow you to build strength, reach more constituents, make communications more easily translatable into other languages, and ultimately enhance your credibility within your community.

As we delve into the development of a system of communication, we must first ensure a shared understanding of the available communication strategies that could be used to support this goal.

PURPOSE OF COMMUNICATION

Communication is a broad and somewhat ambiguous concept. As a school superintendent, there are many items or actions you need to communicate. These may include the following:

- Delivering information about upcoming events
- Sharing detailed information about new programs or opportunities
- Giving accolades, celebrating successes and the various achievements of students, staff, and members of the school community
- Sharing health and safety processes and protocols (thanks, COVID-19!)
- Providing progress updates on major district/school initiatives
- Outlining planned changes to a district program or approach
- Providing community updates about the budget, and/or budget development

If used effectively, a communication strategy can support the implementation of your initiatives. In truth, ineffective or nonexistent communication can result in derailing your intention to make a change you thought was necessary. In your attempt to inform constituents of something important, you may unintentionally devalue the intended change by miscommunicating.

Conversely, if you have communicated effectively, you may successfully reduce the amount of opposition to an initiative or change with a clear and focused message. As a result, your communication may help the community process a pending change better—the focus will remain on the effort for change and not the means of communication.

Is the Communication Technical or Adaptive?

It may be helpful to categorize your communication items based on the concept of "technical" or "adaptive." In "A Survival Guide for Leaders," Ronald Heifetz and Marty Linsky mention the high-stakes risks associated with leaders making changes within an organization.[2] In an organization like a school system, technical problems can be readily solved by applying the know-how of the school system's already established processes.

Adaptive problems are more challenging to tackle because they require more individuals throughout an organization to alter their ways. In other words, adaptive means that solutions to problems lie with *people* changing their behaviors, which we know is not always easy to do.

While the concept of adaptive versus technical is more typically found in discussions around problem solving, this is a helpful framework to adopt and adapt around communication behaviors. Using Heifetz and Linsky's concept, technical items to communicate (e.g., the time of a community meeting, congratulations on a student theatrical production) are typically one-time or informational items that do not require a deeply strategic, multitiered approach to effectively communicate.

What is needed to be successful with these items is the assurance that the message was clear, concise, and delivered at a time and by a means that was received by the intended audience. For adaptive items, the complexity and planning to effectively communicate is amplified significantly. You must plan a specific communication strategy to share information with impacted stakeholders, over time, to support their understanding of the change while garnering additional support for the change.

A communication strategy for an adaptive item should be paired with a project timeline so that you can plan communications of project milestone events. When paired together, this significantly improves the communication of the adaptive item.

ESTABLISHING A CADENCE

Has your practice been to communicate when the mood strikes? When you have cleared enough off your desk to get to it? Or maybe when an issue has increased in urgency and some type of communication becomes a requirement? If you answered yes to any of these questions, it is time to think about establishing a formal and reliable cadence of communication.

So what do we mean by "cadence"? Cadence is simply the expected schedule you will adhere to when communicating. It will also include the people with whom you will be communicating. An expected cadence will support an effective communication strategy for your leadership of the district. Taking the time to define a cadence of communication will create clarity within your district about expected deadlines and necessary preparations for communications internally.

For your community, establishing a cadence of communication is also very important. It will provide your stakeholders with an understanding of when they can expect communication from the district and/or schools. If this plan is communicated ahead of time, and if it is followed, it will serve to protect your district because community members will be able to rely on your timeline and method of communication.

Further, over time, your community will begin to trust you as the superintendent and come to understand what information you will communicate, and under what circumstances. Doing this will improve your effectiveness at managing the multiple complex messages that you are communicating to a wide range of constituent groups.

When thinking about communication, it is helpful to visualize a rock being dropped in a pond. When the rock first hits the pond, the circle of impact is relatively small. And then concentric circles are formed and begin to expand with ever-widening rings around the initial impact of the dropped rock. Now imagine your communication strategy using this metaphor. Each concentric circle represents a different constituent group with whom you are trying to communicate.

The first circle are those closest to the decision and the communication plan—building and central office leaders. The next circle would be faculty and staff, and so on. As you consider this metaphor, think about where constituent groups would be situated.

To put this framework into action, think about a change that you need to communicate. Let's imagine that a district goal is to identify new preK–5 literacy programs and resources needed for use in your district. As you plan for this complex change process, which will likely include concrete action steps to successfully implement this change, you should simultaneously develop a communication timeline. As discussed above, with a pre-established cadence of communication, the communication plan for this change will fit easily into the framework. Think about the following groups to directly and deliberately communicate with:

- Leadership team
- Faculty/staff
- School board
- Students
- Parents
- Entire community

DETERMINING THE BEST METHOD OF COMMUNICATION

So far we have covered many elements of communication. Perhaps the most obvious that we have not yet discussed is determining the appropriate method of communication. As you were reading this chapter, you might have been considering different approaches to communication, or perhaps you were only considering written communication. Either way, it is important to think about the broad range of communication strategies that you have to consider. This includes written communication, of course, but should also include in-person, face-to-face communication.

When to Talk versus Write

There are obvious benefits of using written communication to share important messages. Written communication is easier to share with more people more quickly. Written communication can provide a consistent message that does not change, can be constructed on a schedule that is more convenient for the sender, and takes much less time than in-person sharing. However, a communication plan that does not include opportunities to engage in face-to-face communication does not harness the real power of effective communication.

While more time-consuming, in-person communication provides you with the opportunity to discuss an important item, while better understanding the concerns and questions that an individual or a group might have about a particular topic. You, of course, know this. You have experienced the magnified power of a face-to-face conversation over an expertly crafted email. Your challenge will be to identify the time and setting to provide opportunities for in-person communication.

The Case of Social Media: To Tweet or Not to Tweet, That Is the Question

Many of us who enter the role of superintendent can remember back to the time before social media existed. Some of us would love to put this genie back in the bottle and return to those pre–social media, uninformed Luddite days. Unfortunately, that is not possible. While social media is a relatively new phenomenon, with Facebook being founded in 2004, Twitter in 2006, and Instagram in 2010, there is still so much to learn.

At the dawn of the social media phenomenon, these platforms offered the promise of enhanced communication for families and friends to stay connected or to improve connections among professional groups. Information could be easily shared. Ahh, how naive we all were back then. What we didn't realize at the inception of the social media phenomenon was how *misinformation* could also be so easily spread.

In the years since their founding, we have seen an expansion of both users and uses for social media platforms. Essential to the superintendent's role has been the use of social media to share information and promote activities within the school community. When and if used effectively, social media can elevate the profile of your district and enhance communication.

As school superintendent, you must act immediately to predetermine the use of social media within your district. While your district likely has some pre-existing behaviors around social media, as you enter the school district it is important that you restate the purpose and use of social media in your district. To do this, you should meet with your district leadership team, including your communications director (if you have a communications director). In that meeting you should consider the following:

- Social media use goals
- Social media credentials and use
- Social media channels
- Your personal/professional social media presence

Social Media Use Goals

What is your goal in using social media? Many school districts use social media for a wide variety of purposes. You must decide what your purpose is. When considering your school district's purpose in using social media, consider how you will use social media platforms to broaden the reach of the regular district and school communications (e.g., weekly newsletters). Think about how your district will use social media to provide followers a look inside your school buildings as you highlight excellent practices.

Will you use social media to provide followers with information on special events and activities (e.g., a visit from the local zoo to an elementary school)? Will you use social media to share reminders and information about upcoming activities and events (e.g., a high school theater production)? How will your district use social media to actively engage, or not, with followers who tag or direct message these accounts? Connected to this is the deliberate decision about whether accounts will allow comments and direct messages at all.

Social Media Credentials and Use

You will also need to determine if you will share the burden of continuing to allow your school district to be active on social media. You will need to decide who will have the authority to post on behalf of the district, or the individual school. Will you leverage multiple district administrators to support enhancements of messages, and what will be the frequency of messages on your social media feeds? Do you want the social media messages to come from one entity or person, or is it okay for information to come from multiple entities or people?

You must also determine the "use case" for social media. Since our work includes students, you must verify that the district leadership team clearly understands what is allowed when it comes to posting on social media regarding students. Is there a policy around student pictures that will inform this decision? What has been the past practice related to posting student learning inside the school? Will you allow posts of social/extracurricular events only? What limits will you set to ensure the protection of your students?

Social Media Channels

It is likely that your school district uses some official social media channels. As you engage in planning around social media, you will need to determine if there are other social media platforms that you will add to the list. You will need to consider the logistics of posting, as well as adopting a tool that will allow you to post to multiple social media channels simultaneously. This will allow you to maximize your reach with the greatest level of efficiency.

An important consideration is social media use and your students. Be sure that you understand each social media platform and the allowable minimum age of use and communicate those expectations. You want to avoid a situation where students are encouraged to use an app they are technically not old enough to use.

Your Personal/Professional Social Media Presence

It should go without saying that, as school superintendent, you no longer have the benefit of a "personal" social media account. Even with all of the privacy settings engaged, you should never assume that a private post is ever really private. In your new superintendent role, you must post with caution.

If you haven't already done so, it is also recommended that you take a walk down memory lane and check that your previous posts will not stir controversy. Some school superintendents have lost their jobs (and livelihood) over a personal post that created concern and controversy within the community. Always remember that if a post you have made would cause embarrassment or require explanation in your district, then you should not post it. *Ever*.

In addition to determining how you will engage in the use of your "personal" social media accounts, you must also decide how you are going to use your professional accounts on social media. You may have already adopted a use pattern with social media channels. This pattern may have provided you with an opportunity to engage other professionals. Perhaps you used these channels to celebrate the success of your district in your previous role. Or maybe you have not been active on social media.

Whatever path you have chosen, it is time to reassess your use of social media. You will need to determine how your personal social media streams will be used in light of your new role. Will you echo or reshare posts that are shared via official social media channels? Will you use your accounts to share an inside look into your role and responsibility? Or will it be somewhere in between? Will you actively engage with mentions or messages from your community? When deciding these things, you should determine how much time you will spend, and your level of comfort, on social media.

A word of caution here—too often, superintendents new to their position may be overzealous or try to do it all. Remember that the behaviors you engage in online as the superintendent when you begin the new position will be difficult to undo as you learn more about the challenges of keeping up with your self-imposed commitments. Imagine setting yourself up to post a congratulatory message to every athletic team that wins a game, and then missing some.

Always remember that the use of social media should enhance, not *be*, your leadership messages and strategy. After all, the work of keeping a district's social media channel or channels active, combined with managing your own social media accounts, will be a never-ending challenge.

CONCLUSION

Effective communication as a school superintendent will require persistent, planned, and evolving practices. Establishing systems of communication will support the development of school district norms that your community can come to rely on from your communication. When you engage in communication, you should keep the following in mind:

- *Students first.* Always use an opportunity to communicate to discuss how the issue, change, or problem is impacting students. Focus on the student experience and the need to support them.
- *Core values.* You should leverage all communication channels to share your core values within your messaging. The reinforcement of your core values to your community will continue to support your work.
- *Write with care.* When writing, be sure that your messages convey care, empathy, and thoughtfulness. While you will likely be dealing with dozens or hundreds of emails each day, take the time necessary to convey these attributes.
- *Communication rules.* Adopt some communication rules that you will adhere to. For example, be sure to respond to all phone calls within twenty-four hours and email messages within forty-eight hours.
- *Friday communications.* There is a natural tendency to wrap up the work week by completing some specific tasks, like sending out email communication. Too often when doing so, you create a situation where any responses to the communication you sent will not be dealt with until the following week. Or worse, you spend time over the weekend sending responses. Don't send communications on Fridays!
- *Follow through.* Be sure to follow through on the actions outlined in your communication. This builds trust.

- *Get help.* As necessary, use the existing communications director (if you have one), or work with a communications consultant to help shape messages that are going to be powerful and supportive of the work you are doing.

You will likely spend much more time engaged in communication—of all forms—than you expected. The obligation to communicate regularly and effectively, added to all the other responsibilities, will become overwhelming. There will be a time when you ask yourself if this level of communication is necessary and worth it. It absolutely is. Be sure to continue to prioritize the importance of regular communication to your community. You may not see it directly, but that communication will pay off.

EXPERIENCES FROM THE FIELD

I learned, through some very challenging circumstances, that to effectively manage change, you have to manage information. An important practice that we have adopted has been to include a communication and feedback plan with any strategic change processes that the district is engaged in.

A few years ago we recognized that the tracking system at our middle school was not a model that supported a renewed focus on equity. We worked to establish a clear pathway to dig into this issue and move forward with a change. We launched a steering committee to review relevant research and compare "best practices" to our practice. Not surprisingly, the recommendation was to de-track our middle school.

Importantly, while we were engaged in studying the issue, we also frequently communicated to the community where we were in the process. We offered opportunities to offer feedback and opinions about a potential change. We identified an implementation plan that would be tiered and start with grade 6 and move up each year with that group of students.

The spring prior to the school year that the new de-tracked system went into effect, the middle school principal was conducting a meeting with incoming grade 6 parents. The principal shared lots of orientation information with families and also shared the structure of classes that no longer included academic levels. There were a few questions. It was clear that the communication path chosen was effective in informing and engaging families about this change. We thought it was a great success.

ADDITIONAL RESOURCES

DeSieghardt, Kenneth S. *School Communication That Works: A Patron-Focused Approach to Delivering Your Message*. Lanham, MD: Rowman & Littlefield, 2013.

Heath, Chip, and Dan Heath. *The Power of Moments: Why Certain Experiences Have Extraordinary Impact*. New York: Simon & Schuster, 2017.

Magette, Kristin. *Embracing Social Media: A Practical Guide to Manage Risk and Leverage Opportunity*. Lanham, MD: Rowman & Littlefield, 2014.

Sanfelippo, Joseph M., and Tony Sinanis. *The Power of Branding: Telling Your School's Story*. Thousand Oaks, CA: SAGE Publications, 2014.

Chapter 8

I Need Help!

Using Your Network

EXPERIENCES FROM THE FIELD

As a new assistant superintendent going to my first state superintendents/assistant superintendents conference, I didn't know anyone. I remember feeling like a fish out of water, and somewhat stressed out, attending my first few superintendent conferences alone.

Over time I started to talk to more people around me, attend more workshops, meet others, and begin to socialize with an expanding cohort of peers. Soon after I began to put myself out there and tried to be more outgoing, I began to feel more accepted. This made me feel like I belonged with these accomplished professionals, and more comfortable to be myself while learning and sharing with peers.

Now with a decade of experience as a superintendent and assistant superintendent, I see these conferences more as a respite where I can continue to make myself better in my profession, but also to connect with colleagues who have become friends. I look forward to these times when we can learn from each other, unwind, and take a short break from the daily challenges that we face each day at work in our districts.

This has also reminded me to reach out and connect with others new to the superintendent or assistant superintendent role. Like other, more experienced superintendents who have helped me in the past, I want to return the favor in the present.

GETTING AND GIVING HELP AS A SUPERINTENDENT

Veteran school superintendents should be experienced in both receiving assistance from other superintendents, as well as giving help to their superintendent colleagues. When times get tough, superintendents can feel quite alone and desperate for help. For a new or veteran superintendent, great power comes with a collegial network to support and inspire each other.

Sometimes all the help superintendents need is to have someone relatable hear their problems, serve as a true confidant to just be there and listen, or lift their spirits with companionship. Whether it be a challenging personnel problem, a communication issue with other city or town leaders, budget issues, a union grievance, or perhaps even a personal problem unrelated to the superintendency role, superintendents need people to be there for them, provide nonjudgmental advice, and calmly let them know that "this too shall pass."

When superintendents feel desperate, and don't know if they can do it any longer, they need a network of colleagues to turn to, seek advice from, and build confidence in the idea that they can overcome these challenges to continue to do important work for their students.

We Know More Collectively Than We Do Individually

Let's be honest—the road to the superintendency includes great career success, and a bit of confidence that you were the right person for the job. Sometimes that success can result in superintendents feeling that they need to have all the answers and know exactly how to handle every situation. The truth is, that expectation is impossible. We all benefit from those who have served before us and those who are serving with us.

Successful superintendents have attained their educational leadership positions not just because of what they have accomplished themselves, but also because of those who have served them in the past by providing guidance and mentorship in their development as a leader. Knowing others who have held similar positions, share similar core values, and understand the complexity of the superintendent role is certainly beneficial.

As a principal, calling someone who has already dealt with a similar principal problem can help, just like a curriculum director or assistant superintendent calling someone who has dealt with a similar situation can help provide context for solving that particular problem. The same applies for school superintendents. Other superintendents understand the problem(s) you are dealing with like no one else can. It is important for superintendents to reach out to colleagues outside of their district who may be able to explain the pros and cons of how they dealt with a similar situation in the past.

We Need to Support One Another

School superintendents must be available to aid and support each other, perhaps now more than ever. Many superintendents can, and will, burn out.

Job-alike colleagues working in such unique and complex positions require support, assistance, and encouragement from their peers. With no other true "job-alikes" in each district, superintendents need people in the same position to talk to, vent with, and turn to for guidance, advice, and camaraderie.

Superintendents will often gravitate toward other superintendents at functions or events because of the ease they may feel knowing they are in the company of someone they can relax with, and understands the deep and complex work of the superintendency. Whether it be a fellow practicing superintendent, retired superintendent, or perhaps a partner at home, superintendents need someone who can listen in a nonjudgmental way, allow the superintendent's vulnerabilities to manifest, and then help the superintendent move forward in a constructive way without resenting aspects of the job that can get messy or be unpleasant to handle.

Providing Assistance

Like former NBA players John Stockton or Magic Johnson, or more current NBA players such as Chris Paul or Rajon Rondo, we need to provide good "dimes," or assists, to fellow superintendents. Superintendent colleagues should be seen as allies helping their peers, not as competitors. Superintendents should be rooting for other school superintendents to be successful.

Ultimately, a fellow superintendent's success and ideas will support our continued improvement. When a superintendent colleague reaches out for something, you should make it a priority to help them. When another superintendent shares a problem they are experiencing, or asks whether you have dealt with something similarly challenging, you should listen with empathy, think of how you can help, and provide them with the assistance they need.

FROM SUPERINTENDENT SOLITUDE TO A SUPERINTENDENT NETWORK

Having likely spent time in previous school leadership positions such as assistant principal, principal, assistant superintendent, or chief financial officer, superintendents are used to spending some time alone. Being alone should be perfectly fine for any superintendent personality type.

Even if a superintendent does not enjoy solitude, or prefers to be in the company of others, they should try not to worry too much about spending time alone as the district leader. Furthermore, it should not be shameful for a superintendent to feel alone or estranged; feeling this way is perfectly normal.

But school superintendents should be careful not to spend *too* much time alone. Superintendents who spend too much time in their offices, or spend the majority of their time with their central office staff or with school committee members, may lose touch with the real work happening in the classrooms.

Besides spending invaluable time with students and teachers in classrooms, and principals in school hallways, superintendents should try spending time with superintendent colleagues from other districts in their region. Superintendents who are true lifelong learners will want to learn from some of their more experienced peers, in particular.

Lessening the Loneliness

For a superintendent, loneliness at work can be a very real problem, but successful superintendents will adapt to their circumstances and deal with the most isolating aspects of the job in a positive way. A benefit of the sometimes secluded or quiet parts of the superintendent role is that you will likely have fewer disruptions than in most other educational leadership positions you have held.

This "alone time" can be beneficial for a superintendent to self-reflect, create, strategically think or plan how to lead into the future, or simply ruminate on a problem of practice. If you were previously a principal, you know how sacred this uninterrupted time can be, since most principals are constantly inundated with daily challenges that can too easily change the trajectory of their best-intentioned plans or days.

Join Professional Organizations

One of the best ways to stay current with educational trends, research, and opportunities is to make sure you are a part of a professional superintendent organization. Most superintendents should have paid memberships to local, state, and national superintendent associations as part of their superintendent contracts. School superintendents should include, as part of their practice, reviewing the various publications from these professional organizations. Superintendents can use these readings to further their knowledge and also share applicable information with their respective district leadership teams.

Attend Workshops and Conferences

Superintendents should attend professional conferences. Most connected superintendents will attend professional conferences each year, perhaps one national and one at the state level. Some superintendents may attend closer to four or five conferences depending on the organization(s) and topics being explored at the conferences. If a superintendent's school board questions why their superintendent wants to or needs to attend conferences or workshops, the superintendent should speak to their school board about the professional and personal value in learning from professionals who work outside of the district. Inexperienced school superintendents in particular cannot improve without learning from more experienced school superintendents.

Network

The learning that takes place in sessions while attending conferences is very beneficial. Equally important—or perhaps even more important—are the connections made with colleagues and the informal discussions superintendents engage in with their peers. Whether it be impromptu conversations with a colleague over lunch, or even a quick phone conversation, a spark can be created to positively impact a superintendent's leadership practices by networking. You may have a new idea, or a new solution to a problem that has been hanging around. Superintendents should seek out colleagues they can learn from and connect with.

You can create your own professional learning opportunities by hosting or participating in some roundtable sessions, virtual or in person, and engaging in problems of practice where superintendents collaborate. This gives superintendents opportunities for feedback regarding how they would handle a particular situation.

Social gatherings may also take place where superintendents can simply chat with fellow superintendents who may also want to connect. Many experienced school superintendents also choose to meet with other school superintendents during their personal time.

Socialize and Bond

If a superintendent attending a conference wants to retreat to their room to catch up on sleep or take solace in some much-needed down time, they should go for it! But they shouldn't do this for the entire conference. A superintendent should use conference time as an opportunity to meet new people, bond with other superintendents or assistant superintendents, and connect with colleagues.

Even the most veteran and seasoned superintendents can be shy or experience social anxiety when forced to mingle or meet new people, which can be especially intimidating among a group of other established superintendents. Like superintendents would ask of their students and staff, they should be vulnerable, take risks, and put themselves out there without stressing too much about what others think. Superintendents worry about what others think enough in the day-to-day work within their districts, anyway.

Identify and Confide in Your Trusted Colleagues

From joining professional organizations, networking, and socializing, you should have identified some trusted colleagues who are friends, or at least are friendly enough for you to connect with further. You should be able to exchange cell phone numbers with these people, call or text as needed, meet for coffee, and/or further collaborate.

Connected superintendents should not hesitate to pick up the phone to ask a colleague for advice, bounce ideas off, or perhaps share a "you're not going to believe this" funny story from time to time. Many school superintendents will develop trusting and lasting relationships with other superintendents once they start to realize they are not alone, and these relationships can often lead to lifetime friendships with a network of trusted colleagues.

Ask Questions for Advice

It's tough as a school superintendent to admit that you don't know something. The reality of your role is that many of the challenges may be out of your comfort zone, or in areas where you have limited background (e.g., school finance). Training in educational leadership only gets you so far. To delve further into effective problem solving, a superintendent must not be afraid to ask others for help. *Who* a superintendent asks for help is critical and should be carefully considered as you develop your network.

Generally, a superintendent should ask questions of those who came before them. The people they ask would ideally have some experience in the school superintendent role or serve as a mentor or superintendent coach. Asking others within the school district for help can sometimes be beneficial, but superintendents need to be aware that people within their district may only be able to see things from their respective roles or experience. They may also see the superintendent as weak or unqualified if they think the question the superintendent asks is easy to answer. For example, a superintendent may have a trusted subordinate who works for them, such as a business manager or principal, but these individuals may provide advice primarily from their finance or school-based perspective. A superintendent also needs to be aware that someone who works for them may provide answers to their superintendent's question as a subordinate, not necessarily as a peer or confidant.

Depending on the school superintendent's relationship with school board members, it may *sometimes* be appropriate to ask individual board members for advice, but the superintendent should know that school board members may also perceive this solicitation for advice as a sign of weakness, an invitation to become involved in day-to-day decision making, or, even worse, a breach of confidentiality. Superintendents should be careful not to discuss personnel issues or give individual board members too much of a say in things that may be outside of their purview.

Share Successes

When afforded the opportunity, it is important for a school superintendent to share with colleagues what you do well in your district. In sharing successes, you are helping other superintendents learn about things that you have already been able to accomplish in your district and passing on your experience. This sharing of best practices can, in turn, help fellow superintendents replicate programming in their districts that may benefit more students. Most successful school superintendents have been able to use something they learned from colleagues by replicating or recycling an idea or practice, and then match it with their particular school district.

In sharing successes, an important caveat is to not act like a know-it-all or act like "the way *I* do it" or "the way *we* do it" is better than or superior to other ways. Avoid making it seem like your practices as a superintendent are the best, because even if your idea or way of doing things is great for your particular setting, that practice may not match the school district of the superintendent colleague(s) you are advising. Remember that no one likes a braggart. Don't preach—teach.

MUST-DO STRATEGIES FOR A NEW OR VETERAN SUPERINTENDENT

In addition to the first-year plans of action outlined in the first chapter of this book, such as participating in a new superintendent induction program, establishing an entry plan, and communicating your core values, superintendents new to a school district should engage in the following strategies. Collectively, these can serve as a blueprint for how new or veteran school superintendents can expand their professional network, improve their skill set, lessen the loneliness of the superintendent job, and increase their sphere of influence.

Work Closely with Your District Leadership Team

District leadership team members are an extension of the superintendent. It is important for a superintendent to work closely with *all* leadership team members. New superintendents should be sure to listen to school and district administrators who have been in the district for many years to get a historical perspective. Some school superintendents may focus most of their attention and spend the majority of their time with just the central office leadership team members; this is a mistake. Superintendents need to spend considerable time connected to where the real work is—in the schools and the classrooms with principal and assistant principal leadership team members.

Themes will emerge in the schools and the classrooms that a superintendent can see, hear, count, and categorize. Superintendents should work with the principals they evaluate to help them create and refine their individual goals and school improvement goals, which should be connected to district improvement goals. Staying focused on principals' instructional leadership practices will let them know that high-impact instructional practices is your main priority as the superintendent of schools.

There should be nothing more important than the work happening in the classrooms between the teachers and their students. Staying engaged through classroom walkthroughs with school principals lets everyone know the school superintendent cares and is focused on teaching and learning. Through this process, superintendents should also get a sense of what teachers need to improve their practices. You will also learn which teachers are high performing; knowing this information should encourage a superintendent to coach principals to use the educator evaluation process to try to help struggling educators get better, and also grow teacher-leaders to become potential school and district leaders of the future.

Work with a Coach or Mentor

Being able to honestly speak with someone who can objectively provide assistance and advice is crucial for a school superintendent to survive and thrive. As previously described, a new superintendent mentor or coach can be used as part of a new superintendent induction program. If not through an induction program, a superintendent coach can be recommended by another superintendent or personally selected by the superintendent.

Many experienced superintendents will work formally with "executive coaches" to continue to help them refine their skills, leadership behaviors, and practices. These relationships typically include regularly scheduled meetings, with the ability to reach out via a phone call as needed.

Mentors or coaches can walk superintendents through situational leadership dilemmas they may be experiencing, use protocols to help explore problems of practice, or simply meet to listen to the problems the school superintendent may be encountering. Mentors and coaches can listen impartially, provide sound judgment, and help a superintendent make decisions in the best interest of students. The support of a mentor or coach who is objective, and has applicable experience, will provide excellent support to the new superintendent.

Be Kind and Approachable, and Show Gratitude toward Other Superintendents

Think back to when you were a new teacher. Do you remember encountering a few colleagues who were experienced and who genuinely wanted to help you be successful in your role as a teacher? You should seek out the same as a new superintendent. Isn't it great when you meet a colleague who is approachable, nice, relatable, and thankful for your friendship and time? These are the superintendent colleagues you should gravitate toward, as they can lift you up and help you improve.

School superintendents should want to be around other superintendents who can serve as mentors or make them better in their profession. There is nothing better than meeting another superintendent with shining eyes who seems to like you and wants to relate to and help you. Conversely, we've all met pompous superintendents who seem to know it all, do not want to socialize with you because they may view you as inexperienced or inferior, or who seemingly thinks they are above your presence. Avoid that type of superintendent and look for those who are open and interested.

Remember to pay it forward. Help superintendents in need. Be kind to *all* colleagues. Being a superintendent is a regularly humbling experience. The role keeps you consistently grounded. Spend as much time conversing with all of the staff—custodians, administrative assistants, cafeteria workers, and instructional aides—as you do with teachers, principals, assistant superintendents, superintendents, and school board members. In your interactions with others, come from a place of care. Show that you want to help others, just as many people in your past prior to your tenure as a superintendent have helped you.

Promote Positivity

School superintendents are district and community leaders who should promote a positive outlook on the work of the school district. This involves not just speaking positively, but even more importantly, modeling upbeat and optimistic attitudes through behaviors. Negative narratives can easily spread and run rampant, especially through social media, so superintendents should take the lead by trying to flip any negative scripts through their actions. Remember to enter situations with questions and optimism, not negativity.

Positive mindsets usually emerge when people feel a connection to their work environment. People crave human connection. This is why it is important to promote genuine collaboration among staff. Helping to build relationships reduces stress and isolation, can further the potential of the individuals and groups within the district, and promote a more positive work environment.

School superintendents can first model this work with their leadership teams, then follow up and participate alongside school-based professional learning communities or smaller groups of faculty.

All school superintendents will inevitably experience scrutiny and backlash at times, sometimes warranted and sometimes unwarranted. Although superintendents need to continue to lead and not succumb to pressure, superintendents must also resist the urge to push back too aggressively. Keeping your composure and displaying integrity will be respected by those watching and paying attention. Superintendents need to keep a positive mindset and take the high road even when others do not. Showing anger and impatience will be perceived as a sign of weakness. As the old adage warns: Never mud wrestle with a pig because you'll both get dirty, but only one of you will like it.

CONCLUSION

Working well with others is essential for any school superintendent to survive. Besides working with constituents within a superintendent's city or town and school district, it is important for superintendents to seek outside colleagues to get help, share ideas, and be there for support. A collegial superintendent should not just get help, but also be willing to give help. We are all in this together.

One single superintendent can only do and know so much. Effective superintendents should surround themselves with a network of peers to expand their influence and gain knowledge from other experienced superintendents. Staying connected with other leaders both inside and outside of your school district should lessen loneliness and bolster a superintendent's sense of purpose. It is imperative for new as well as experienced superintendents to use mentors, keep a positive mindset, and behave in ways that will encourage and inspire others.

EXPERIENCES FROM THE FIELD

When I was the new superintendent, I exerted 100 percent of my energy to the work on the ground in my school district. Once I started to feel a sense of burnout from the nonstop pace of the new job, I turned to some of my superintendent colleagues who could relate to the trials and tribulations I was experiencing. During this time, I felt there was instant camaraderie with the other superintendents who seemed to know exactly what I was dealing with. I soon realized there was great value from leaning on others who were going through similar situations.

Through collaboration with fellow school superintendents, I have learned that the best superintendents seem to be those who look toward others to make themselves better. Besides the typical venting to colleagues, I have learned so many "best practices" from other superintendents who have helped me in my role as superintendent of schools, as well as an educational leader.

ADDITIONAL RESOURCES

Creasman, Brian, Bernadine Futrell, and Trish Rubin. *ConnectED Leaders: Network and Amplify Your Superintendency*. Lanham, MD: Rowman & Littlefield, 2019.

Fette, J. "Superintendents Who Network: What Do They Value about Participation in a Peer Network?" Doctoral dissertation, The Ohio State University, 2018. https://etd.ohiolink.edu/apexprod/rws_etd/send_file/send?accession=osu1523400238136514&disposition=inline.

Pardini, P. "Executive Coaching," American Association of School Administrators. Accessed January 2, 2023. https://www.aasa.org/SchoolAdministratorArticle.aspx?id=8952.

Chapter 9

The Sky Is Falling!

Leading through Challenges and Crises

EXPERIENCES FROM THE FIELD

The high school principal informed me that there had been a physical fight in the hallway during passing time. Thankfully no one was hurt. The three students who were involved were being dealt with by the assistant principals, and their parents were heading to the high school to pick them up. I thanked her and continued with my day.

A few hours later I received a phone call from a member of the school committee who was concerned about the fight at the high school. I provided additional details about the situation and assured her that the principal was managing the situation. The work day came to an end and I headed home.

Later that evening I received a panicked call from the high school principal. She shared that some students took video of the fight and posted it on social media. To further complicate matters, there was an allegation that one of the students had a weapon. We decided that the best course would be to send out an email to the high school community. We worked together on a statement that she put out to the community.

The next morning I had a dozen emails from upset parents. They were upset about the situation and the communication timeline in particular. Many of the emails were from families who did not have students at the high school, who had heard about the situation. The principal and I spent much of that day calling families and explaining the situation, sharing my apologies, and sending out an updated statement to the entire district. From that point forward, I have made it a habit to practice timely communication to the school and district community when situations like this occur.

PROBLEMS, CHALLENGES, AND CRISES . . . OH MY!

As a school administrator, you are well acquainted with challenging and difficult circumstances. The range is wide—from challenging student behaviors, problematic personnel, upset parents, and community outrage about a decision that was made. More recent is the dramatically increased level of concern from the community over the current, polarized political atmosphere.

Schools have been pulled into the middle of the political division and many previously unchallenged, and relatively benign, decisions are being scrutinized with a new level of zeal and interest. This is a recipe for a daily onslaught of challenges, problems, and crises that will require sustained attention.

Despite the nature of any concern, whether lower-level or more significant, each situation must be managed effectively, efficiently, transparently, and respectfully, either by an educational leader or by the school superintendent. Unfortunately, if these circumstances are not dealt with effectively, they will compound or grow. The proverbial molehill will become the mountain. As the low-level concern turns into a more significant crisis, *you* will be forced to step in and assist in managing the situation. The impact of this late start and the inability to manage the situation at a lower level will be significant and will come at the cost of your time, attention, and focus.

While managing challenging situations is always difficult, the impact will be even more problematic if these are not well handled at the outset. Your focus on teaching and learning will suffer. Your primary work with students will be deeply affected as you will now need to turn your attention to a more urgent, conflict-related matter—that in some cases may have been preventable.

From your previous position to your new position as school superintendent, there has been an important change in the area of managing challenges and crises that you may not have yet recognized. As superintendent of schools, the quantity and intensity of problems will grow exponentially. You are, after all, where the buck stops and, for the majority of issues, the individual in the district who often has final decision-making authority in most situations.

As you start your new role as superintendent, it is important that you establish a clear understanding for those around you about what you expect from their management of difficult situations. You will need to verify that your subordinates and your supporters understand your expectations (and tolerance) around potential challenges.

- Do you want a principal to call you anytime they have had a difficult conversation with a parent that may lead to your office?

- Do you want school board members to inform you of the community dialogue around important issues?
- When and how do you want to be informed about an emerging crisis—at any time, including evenings or weekends?
- Do you want parent liaisons to make you aware of the latest social media outrage that is taking place connected to your district?

The answers to these questions are important, as they will guide those around you to determine the steps to take when an issue is simmering before it comes to a full boil. Your constituents' clear understanding of your expectations will support the effective management of these challenges and prevent them from mushrooming into more significant issues. Your subordinates and supporters' understanding of your expectations will also build their leadership capacity and strength in managing challenging situations.

Should I Manage the Issue or Support Others?

This is another critical question. Your natural instinct will be to step in and fix the problem. After all, you are a problem solver who gets things done. This problem-solving ability is likely part of the reason that you moved into this important role of school superintendent. The problem-solving gene seems to be embedded within the DNA of most educational leaders—especially when they are working to solve other people's problems. How will you behave when issues are brought to you?

One challenge that many educational leaders, including school superintendents, face is that they like to solve other people's problems. Often their problem-solving behavior includes taking over the situation—after all, they are a leader, right? This is often done to the detriment of other individuals who might be able to solve the problem and who will learn and hone important problem-solving skills. While you may believe that *you* are the most capable problem solver, and this may be true, there is another, unintended message that you are sending to members of your community—that only the school superintendent can solve problems.

This approach will inevitably set up a scenario where members of the community learn about your behavior and believe that all decision making occurs at the top, and that no other individual in your district can help them with their problem. As the word gets out, you will be inundated with smaller issues and challenges that other members of your leadership team can and should resolve. This approach will impact the confidence of leaders and hinder their continued development. The result will be that other leaders will begin bringing all types of concerns to you for advice and solutions.

Imagine a scenario where your high school principal just called to inform you that an assistant principal had a difficult and unproductive conversation with a parent. The conversation did not go well and the parent informed the assistant principal that they would be calling the superintendent immediately. As you consider your options, you think about the impact of trying to solve this challenge. If you choose to become involved, you will have undermined (unintentionally, of course) the authority of the building principal.

You have also set up an expectation for this parent that any issues of importance that arise regarding their children and the school can only be solved if you are involved. On the other hand, if you inform that parent that you are aware of the issue and the building principal will contact them to work through this challenge, you have preserved the principal's authority and sent an important message that the "chain of command" needs to be followed to effectively manage challenges.

Whose Problem Is This?

So, when *should* you take over and manage the issue? As school superintendent, you should ask yourself, "Whose problem is this?" This is a critical question when considering whether or not you should immediately get involved, or coach someone else through a problem-solving scenario that more closely involves them. Some guidance about when you *should* get involved and take over includes the following:

- *Unproductive conversations.* When a situation at a lower level, with one of your direct reports, is persistent and continues to remain unresolved, you may consider becoming involved.
- *The issue has grown.* When the issue has grown to be larger than an individual school, involves multiple schools, and/or has started to gain momentum within the community.
- *Your team made a mistake.* This should be obvious, but when a leadership team member has made a mistake and attempts to resolve the situation unsuccessfully, you will need to get involved. Start by apologizing.
- *School board involvement.* This one is tricky and requires some reflection. If the school board becomes involved in a situation, you may need to become involved in order to protect your leadership team. Depending on the specific situation, you may also plan a follow-up with the school board to debrief this situation to make sure the board members "remain in their lane."
- *The issue is political and persistent.* While all educational leaders have to deal with the local political environment, a situation that has some

roots of a political nature may be best handled and resolved with your involvement.

IS IT A PROBLEM OR A DILEMMA?

When confronted with a challenge, it is helpful to categorize it so that you can work most efficiently to resolve it. Ask yourself, "Is this a problem, or a dilemma?" The answer will help you set a path, and adjust your expectations, for potential outcomes.

A *problem* is often discrete and solvable, although not always to the satisfaction of a community member. Problems are more common than dilemmas, and they will come in significant numbers to your desk. For example, your office receives a request from a parent who would like to start their four-year-old in kindergarten. The school board has a policy about the starting age of the child and prohibits a child who is not five before the start date of school from enrolling. Your decision is to adhere to the policy or make an exception, if permissible. The response to the problem is straightforward and binary in this case.

A *dilemma* is much more complex and often persists without a clear and easy solution. Typically, there may be multiple solutions to a dilemma, but they are not clear or attractive. Decision making around a dilemma may also result in potential solutions that do not align with our core values, but are nonetheless necessary to make. When managing a dilemma we must choose the best solution, but it often does not feel like the right solution. Simply put, the right solution does not exist for a dilemma.

As an example, imagine that you have a scheduled appeal hearing for a long-term suspension of forty-five days for a high school student. The high school principal made the decision to levy a long-term suspension because of an egregious breach of behavioral expectations. As you prepare for the meeting, you learn more about the student and the student's history and circumstances at home that have deeply impacted the child. You learn from the child's guidance counselor that this long-term suspension will likely have a long-term detrimental impact on the child's education. Specifically, you are concerned the child might drop out of school.

The dilemma here is clear—as an educator, you are responsible for ensuring that all students have a high-quality learning experience. Further, you have the obligation to break down barriers so that a child has access to an effective education. As the school superintendent, it is also your responsibility to make the learning environment safe and accessible for all students. You find yourself in the unenviable position of deciding between the impact on one child, or the larger school community. Welcome to managing a dilemma.

With this situation, you have a few options, but all will have a likely negative impact on those involved. You could meet and uphold the suspension levied by the principal. As mentioned, this decision may lead to a negative educational outcome for the student—dropping out of school. Upholding the suspension would also send a clear message that speaks to your leadership and community about tolerance for behavioral infractions of this nature.

Another option is to conduct the meeting and reduce the length of the suspension. This will send a message that the behavior was not as serious as the principal indicated. It may also result in a negative reaction from community members who are connected to the issue or who believe that you are not taking the issue seriously enough. In addition, a reduction of the penalty may not change the negative educational outcome for the student.

Finally, you might decide that a different penalty is warranted and decide to overrule the principal and cancel any suspension. This will send multiple messages to the community, other students, and your leadership team. A decision like this could send the message that you do not trust the decision making of your leadership team. This lack of support may foment discord between you and the high school principal. It may also send a message to other students and the school community that the behavior was not serious enough to warrant the significant penalty imposed by the principal.

Whichever decision is made, it is not ideal. It may also conflict with your core values. When you find yourself in a situation like this, it is important to think through all the possible solutions to thoroughly understand the impact of your decision. This is also a good opportunity to talk through the problem with someone who can be more objective and who is not emotionally involved—like a mentor or coach.

WHAT IS A CRISIS?

The answer should be simple, but in reality, it's somewhat complicated. In some ways, a crisis is in the eye of the beholder. In many cases, your action and reaction to a challenge will largely dictate how significant the crisis becomes. The *Merriam-Webster Online Dictionary* defines *crisis* as "an unstable or crucial time or state of affairs in which a decisive change is impending; a situation that has reached a critical phase."[1] As school superintendent, you will find that on a daily basis, multiple issues that meet this definition of a crisis will be brought to you.

Types of Crises

As you review resources on crisis management, you will find some helpful resources categorizing different types of crises. While the examples provided in these resources may not be directly overlaid onto school district leadership, the concepts offer a helpful organizing framework. With this framework, you can plan a management strategy to effectively deal with the crisis.

When faced with a crisis, these categories are helpful in determining potential follow-up to assist in crisis management. Generally, there are three categories of crises: (1) sudden crisis, (2) slow-burn crisis, and (3) creeping crisis.[2] While some resources treat slow-burn and creeping crises as the same, for our purposes it is helpful if they remain separate categories.

The Sudden Crisis

When one thinks of a crisis, a sudden crisis may be the one that comes to mind. A sudden crisis occurs without warning and is the result of a clearly defined precipitating event. A sudden crisis may include natural disasters, a serious bus accident, violent acts committed on school property, or the death of a student or staff member. The discrete and timebound nature of the event, provided that there are no lingering issues, makes this the type of crisis that is technically easiest to prepare for and act on when it occurs. While it occurs without warning, having systems in place to respond will enhance the district's ability to manage the challenge.

The Slow-Burn Crisis

A slow-burn crisis is distinctly different from a sudden crisis. There may be some advance warning of an impending crisis, but it may not be known to school leaders. In some instances, a sudden crisis started as a slow-burn crisis but was not recognized as such. Examples of a slow-burn crisis may include legal action against you and the district, financial challenges around adequately funding the district, or an unsuccessful follow-through to manage a sudden crisis (e.g., a natural disaster that significantly damaged a school building).

The Creeping Crisis

The creeping crisis may be the most difficult to protect against. Similar to the slow-burn crisis, there may have been signs of the looming crisis, but these may have gone unnoticed or seemed unconnected to the larger issue. Think of a creeping crisis as one that persists over a long period of time. For many of us, the challenges around leading schools and districts during the pandemic are a good example of a creeping crisis.

The three types of crises described above are helpful to categorize the crisis you are managing. With that information in mind, you may be able to appropriately adjust your expectations for managing a crisis. Specifically, this information will provide some insight into the length of time the crisis may persist.

MANAGING A CRISIS

Each crisis will offer its own unique challenges. While no two crises will be exactly the same, there are some steps you should put into place to assist you in managing these crises. Specifically, the following questions will help to guide your understanding of the circumstances that led to the crisis and how you might best manage it.

Pre-event

- *Prevention.* What systems, processes, and strategies do you have in place to work toward preventing a crisis from occurring in the first place?
- *Planning and practice.* Do you take time to conduct "table top" exercises to practice potential scenarios, examine deficits, and develop a plan to address the crisis?

During Event

- *Response plan.* Who will be involved in supporting a response plan? Will you engage outside experts to help work with your team to manage the event while underway?
- *Communication.* Who will take primary responsibility for communication during the event? Will it be you or one of your leaders? What process is followed to gain approval for communication from the school or district?

Following Event

- *Post-event follow-up and reflection.* Will you take time to conduct an after-action meeting to debrief the event?

Prevention

An ounce of prevention is worth a pound of cure, or so Benjamin Franklin is credited with saying. The adage is applicable to crisis management. One supportive way to assist you in managing a crisis is to not find yourself in a crisis. Certainly, it is impossible to prevent all crises, but clear systems and expectations will help you avoid some crises. So how can you prevent a crisis? In many scenarios, preventing a simmering issue from becoming a full-blown crisis requires keen observation, quick action, and effectively matching a response to the situation.

Imagine that it is a Friday early afternoon and you are in your office wrapping things up before the weekend. You learn that there is a behavioral situation at your middle school that results in police involvement. The situation involves two students and occurred in the middle school's main office, with only a few students and staff present. As the situation escalated, staff and students were cleared from the office until law enforcement showed up to manage the situation. After a few minutes, the situation de-escalated and the families of both students came to pick up the students.

Your middle school principal calls you to fill you in on the details of the situation. You ask many questions to understand what happened. After some discussion, you both agree that it is not necessary to send out a communication to the school community about the issue. While the situation was momentarily intense, the issue was quickly de-escalated. You confirmed with the principal that the office was clear of unnecessary students and staff. Finally, after a long week, you have been looking forward to getting home to spend some time with your family.

A few hours later, just before shutting down your computer, you see two emails from parents. You know both parents fairly well and often receive emails from them. Both are questioning the events of the day and share their concerns about the overall safety of students. They also share that there is a rumor that both students were arrested. You are running late for dinner and leave for the weekend.

Saturday morning you receive a text from your school board chair and the middle school principal. Rumors about the incident at the middle school continue to circulate overnight. Someone on social media posted that two students were arrested because they brought weapons to school. This results in hundreds of comments, some of which call into question the competence of both you and the middle school principal.

You get the idea—in this scenario, the decision to not send out an email communication to the community created an information void. That void was filled with rumors and innuendo, along with a little pot-stirring on social media. This situation has now become a crisis that requires a plan to address the situation. Of course, all of this might have been prevented with a more proactive approach to the situation.

Planning and Practice

Another important support of crisis management is engaging in regular planning and practice. Whether dealing with a sudden crisis or a crisis of another type, regular planning will be helpful. In most school districts, there are requirements to engage in regular drills and practices. These may include fire drills, tornado drills, and, sadly, lockdown and/or active shooter drills. In addition, there are likely crisis checklists to deal with all manner of emergencies.

While the planning and practice around these issues are important, it does not include all of the potential crises that might befall a school or district. An important consideration for you is determining what other scenarios you should plan and prepare for. These decisions can be highly contextual and related to your community. You should think about the likeliest event and consider a planned response to manage that situation, should it arise.

In addition, you should consider how to prepare your building-based leadership teams to manage a sudden crisis. Look into training opportunities that will support the continued development of your leadership team to prevent and manage crises of all kinds.

Response Plan

As a crisis develops, quick decisions to mitigate the challenge are essential, depending on the nature of the crisis. In many situations, the quick thinking of the principal or other school leader is essential to minimizing the impact of the situation. In some situations, leaders have a tendency to make quick decisions about how to respond to a crisis, even if there is time to take a slower approach. If you have time to come up with a plan, you should use it. This will result in a better response to the crisis and should support a quicker resolution of the situation.

When possible, slow down and make decisions based on all the information available. Gather your team to discuss the crisis and offer feedback about how to manage it. Identify key activities that need to take place, discuss specific steps, and then assign related tasks to members of the team.

Communication

Communication during and following an event is an important part of managing a crisis. Often, there is great demand from the community to know as quickly as possible about what happened, and what the plan is to deal with the situation. Following a crisis, a critical refrain that is often heard is that the communication about the event was slow and incomplete.

Any communication that you can provide during and immediately after the event is helpful in tamping down this criticism. And while none of us like criticism, the purpose of quick, accurate communication about a crisis event is to ensure the entire community has the fact-based information about an event—at the same time.

Post-Event Follow-Up and Reflection

Your responsibility as superintendent to manage all types of challenges and crises has expanded significantly. Another area of responsibility is to take these challenging situations and use them as a tool to build the strength of your team. Conducting an after-crisis review and debrief is a helpful process to better understand what went well and where there were opportunities for improvement. In some cases, sharing the broad results of this type of review to your community is helpful to continue to demonstrate that your district is a reflective and learning organization that strives toward continuous improvement.

CONCLUSION

As superintendent, you will find that you receive a daily dose of impending doom. As your team strives to keep you informed of all the potential crises, you may become overwhelmed. It is important to keep in mind that what you are being presented with on a daily basis are exceptions to the norm. Your early knowledge of potential challenges will allow you to coach your leadership team and strengthen their ability to manage these situations. It will allow you to share your skills and help them build confidence to keep issues off your desk. Over time, the strength of your leadership team in this area will pay dividends as fewer issues will rise to your level.

When they do—and they will—be sure to review them through the lens provided. Is the issue a sudden, slow-burn, or creeping crisis? What strategies can you engage to manage it quickly and effectively? Finally, be sure that you have a communication plan that will provide transparency to members of your community who should be informed of the crisis.

EXPERIENCES FROM THE FIELD

In the early evening of March 13, 2020, I was sitting with a fellow superintendent talking about the events of the day. Earlier that day, we had both announced that our school districts would be closed for a week due to concerns over what was, at that time, a relatively unknown virus. We were both in a state of shock that we had taken this unprecedented action to close our schools. We were not alone. In our state, most district leaders decided to close their schools. Later that weekend, on Sunday, the governor of our state ordered all schools to close for three weeks.

A few weeks later, schools were closed for the remainder of the year. We scrambled to come up with learning plans, deliver devices to students who did not have them, and distribute meals. Little did we know that this was the beginning of a two-year stretch of crisis management. I will never forget the difficulties leaders faced in managing the pandemic, or the important lessons around crisis management that were learned.

ADDITIONAL RESOURCES

Dake, Larry. *Crisis Management: Effective School Leadership to Avoid Early Burnout*. Lanham, MD: Rowman & Littlefield, 2021.

Heifetz, Ronald, and Martin Linsky. *Leadership on the Line: Staying Alive through the Dangers of Change*. Cambridge, MA: Harvard Business Review Press, 2017.

Philpott, Donald, and Paul Serluco. *Public School Emergency Preparedness and Crisis Management Plan*. Lanham, MD: Government Institutes, 2017.

Chapter 10

Pulling It All Together

DOING GOOD THINGS FOR THE STUDENTS YOU SERVE

This final chapter serves as a solutions-oriented summary of this book, which should help any school leader, in particular any school superintendent, to lead with a sense of purpose and direction. The chapter summarizes some key points outlined in each previous chapter, as well as lists specific strategies. All superintendents should be able to readily use these strategies, which are tried and tested, to find success as a superintendent within their school community. While there are many other ideas, strategies, or tactics not found in this book that may work well for school superintendents in their roles, the ones highlighted in this book are a great start for any aspiring, new, or experienced superintendents beginning in a new district.

Throughout this book we offered strategies, ideas, and approaches to ensure that you pay attention to those critical areas that would support your ability to make change. The superintendency will likely be the most challenging position you have ever held. It also is the position that puts you in the driver's seat to move initiatives forward and make improvements in schools, in service to student learning and the student experience.

CONGRATULATIONS, CONDOLENCES, DOS, AND DON'TS

As a superintendent new to a school district, there is a honeymoon period that may last days, weeks, or months—and then reality hits. The role of superintendent is different, yet also similar to other positions you've held as an educational leader. The superintendent job is also more complex than previous positions you've held, but it can be simpler in some ways, too.

There are dos and don'ts for a school superintendent, which include some *must-dos,* such as participating in a new superintendent induction program. Benefits and outcomes from new superintendent induction programs include entry planning, working with an experienced mentor, articulating and communicating your core values, sharing your report of entry findings and goals, soliciting feedback to determine how you can improve relationship building, and determining next steps as you enter year 2. Finally, at the end of year, school superintendents need to *breathe.*

IT'S ALL ABOUT TEACHING AND LEARNING

There should be nothing more important for the school superintendent to focus on than the teaching and learning happening in a district. The superintendent must prioritize the critical work happening between teachers/staff and students. School superintendents need to remember their roots as teachers or educators at heart who still want to help kids.

Much of the work related to teaching and learning is not done by the school superintendents themselves but by others who report to superintendents, or by still others who report to the school principals who answer to the superintendent. Superintendents need to continue to be leaders of instructional improvements and maintain a hyperfocus on teaching and learning above everything else.

Examples of things superintendents can do to keep teaching and learning focused include the following:

- Plan school board meetings that highlight student learning.
- Coach those who need assistance.
- Establish improvement plans that center the teaching and learning experience.
- Align the district budget to focus on supporting student learning.
- Supervise and evaluate principal and district leadership team members.
- Conduct school visits that allow you to visit classrooms with the principal.

Ultimately, school superintendents need to create conditions for their people as educators to do their best work.

NURTURING RELATIONSHIPS WITH SCHOOL BOARD MEMBERS

The importance of relationships with school board members is tantamount to a superintendent's longevity. School board members hire superintendents, and the superintendent needs to report to their board. It is important to note that superintendents work for the school board as a whole, not as individuals. This is an awkward position to be in, as superintendents spend most of their days with staff, students, and families, and a smaller chunk of their time with school board members.

Superintendents need to develop and maintain productive, personal relationships with their school board members. Effective school superintendents need to be able to deal with dissension on their school board, mediate conflict, and also plan to help their school board chair run productive school board meetings to stay focused on fulfilling the needs of all students in the district. Successful school superintendents also need to build relationships and know-how to collaborate with other city or town leaders.

In addition, superintendents must advocate for resources, navigate sometimes muddy or dangerous waters, and mediate issues that arise. Savvy school superintendents should communicate in a variety of ways, hold in-person meetings with board members as much as possible, manage relationships carefully, and at times gently remind individual board members of their role as a school board member.

BUDGET DEVELOPMENT TO IMPROVE STUDENT LEARNING

Any initiative to improve the student experience that you dream up will take up financial resources. You will be able to use those resources by reducing the current costs against the budget, or raise additional funds to allow you to put the new initiative in place. Many new superintendents lack a technical background in school finance that supports a deep understanding of the available funding that may already be included in the budget.

The superintendent can focus on specific strategies to improve their technical understanding of the district budget. Key steps in the process to develop the budget include the following:

- Knowing the multimillion-dollar puzzle—how school districts are funded
- Understanding and implementing a budget development process
- Creating a timeline/budget calendar

- Identifying budget priorities with the leadership team
- Developing the budget proposal with stakeholder engagement
- "Selling" the budget
- Following up to ensure your newly aligned spending priorities are having the impact you planned

BEING OUT AND ABOUT

School superintendents need to develop positive relationships with a number of constituents in the respective city or town where they serve as the educational leader. This is especially important when new to a superintendency and needing to be seen in the community. When interacting with others, it is important for any superintendent to think about how they might make people *feel*.

Most school superintendents started as teachers and wanted to connect with students to help them. Spending time in schools and classrooms should remind the superintendent of their educator roots. Being out and about in the different schools is the best way for a superintendent to experience the real culture of each school.

It is important for a superintendent to show interest in learning from others in their school districts, demonstrating lifelong learning and care for others. Besides conducting school visits, superintendents should attend not only sports events, but also convey interest by riding the school bus, setting up a hallway desk from time to time in each school, and showing up to some other varied extracurricular student events.

Being superintendent isn't really so much about the school leader as it is about the people in the town or city that the superintendent meets with, gets feedback from, and talks to or communicates with. Some things superintendents can do to be visible and stay connected are as follows:

- Attending some city or town council/select board meetings
- Attending town-wide annual events
- Writing handwritten personalized notes

When being seen and building relationships, it is important for the school superintendent to not only convey their sense of purpose, but also ask questions to learn about any perceived strengths, weaknesses, opportunities, or threats that constituents say may be percolating in the school district. By employing empathy and using the knowledge and understanding gained from listening and learning from others who already have experience working in the school district, the strategic superintendent should be able to take action to lead improvements related to teaching and learning.

FROM RECRUITMENT TO RETIREMENT

In the relatively recent past, a posting for a teaching position would result in dozens or hundreds of applicants for most positions. Many districts could simply review submitted applications, put together a hiring committee, and move forward with excellent candidates.

Recently national headlines, especially following the pandemic, have highlighted the impending teacher shortage and the difficulty in filling these roles. As the teacher shortage begins or continues to manifest, you, as superintendent, will be responsible for managing all aspects of the employee experience from recruitment to retirement and everything in between.

You can impact the work culture within your district and schools, and position your district as one that is sought after by would-be applicants. To do this, you need to create a clear plan around human resource practices, including the following:

- Recruitment
- Interview and hiring procedures
- Onboarding new employees
- Assessing and supporting the district and school culture
- Demonstrating care

In addition to putting in place practices that support a high-quality adult culture, you will also be responsible for other aspects of personnel management. Perhaps the most difficult part is managing problematic employees or behavior. It is important that you enter that space with a clear understanding of applicable regulations to make sure that you are treating employees in a fair and consistent manner.

EFFECTIVE COMMUNICATION STRATEGIES

Effective communication as a school superintendent will require persistent, planned, and evolving practices. Establishing systems of communication will support the development of school district norms that your community can come to rely on from your communication. When engaging in communication, you should keep the following in mind:

- Keep the student experience front and center.
- Overcommunicate your core values and connect communications to specific core values.
- When writing, be efficient but thoughtful with the language you are using and the sentiment you are trying to convey.
- Adopt specific rules around communication that are articulated and acted on by all members of your team.
- Don't end the week by sending an actionable communication to staff or the community—it can wait until Monday.
- Be sure to follow up on the promises you make in your communications
- Identify opportunities to get help to improve your messaging in communications.

Communication is a double-edged sword. When done well, you will set an expectation that you effectively convey the important work of the school district to your community. Once that expectation is created, you will find that criticism will abound if you do not meet that expectation. As superintendents get busy, the amount of time spent on communicating will become overwhelming and you will look for opportunities to scale back. Instead, you should find places to get support in writing the communications for the district.

USING YOUR NETWORK

Because we all know more collectively than we do individually, connected school superintendents should be willing to get and also give help to their superintendent colleagues. Superintendents need to support and talk to each other. This will help a superintendent go from a place of solitude to having a real network, which will lessen the loneliness of the job.

Superintendents should be willing to join professional organizations, attend workshops and conferences, network with other educational leaders, and socialize and bond. In addition, school superintendents should try to first identify and then confide in their trusted colleagues, whether they feel the need to ask for advice or share successes. Remember, superintendents are all in this together.

Some must-do strategies for new superintendents include working closely with their district leadership team, using a new superintendent coach or a mentor, promoting positivity, being kind and approachable, and showing gratitude to fellow superintendents.

LEADING THROUGH CHALLENGES AND CRISES

You will quickly learn that a crisis comes in many forms. You will hear about impending challenges, and potential crises, from other members of the leadership team on a daily basis. As superintendent, you will support other leaders who deal with these crises as they occur, or you will manage them yourself. When in these situations, it is important that you have established processes to help you manage the existing crisis.

It is also important to know what type of crisis you are dealing with: sudden, slow-burn, or creeping crisis. Understanding the type of crisis you are dealing with will give you a better sense of how to best match the response strategy to effectively manage the crisis.

An important element of managing a crisis is connected to communication. It is helpful to understand that there will likely always be criticism about the speed and transparency of communication about the crisis. Those impacted by the crisis or the larger community will want to have more information—and more quickly—about the crisis and the district's plan to manage the crisis.

YOU'RE ON YOUR WAY TO GOOD THINGS

We firmly believe that this book can serve as a recipe for success for any aspiring, new, or even veteran school superintendent. If you employ even half the strategies outlined in this guidebook, you will be on your way to a successful tenure as school superintendent in your city or town. Most of the suggestions discussed in these pages are practical and can be used quickly and without too much stress. Now go hit the ground running toward doing great things for the students, staff, families, and community you serve.

Notes

CHAPTER 1

1. "New Superintendent Induction Program," Massachusetts Association of School Superintendents, accessed November 8, 2022, https://www.massupt.org/professional-development/annual-programs/new-superintendent-induction-program/#:~:text=The%20three%2Dyear%20New%20Superintendent,of%20School%20Superintendents%20(MASS).

CHAPTER 3

1. Howard Carlson, "Divided Boards and Dissention," *School Administrator* (February 2022): 10.

CHAPTER 5

1. J. Sanfelippo and T. Sinanis, *Hacking Leadership: 10 Ways Great Leaders Inspire Learning That Teachers, Students, and Parents Love* (Highland Heights, OH: Times 10 Publishing, 2016), p. 15.

CHAPTER 6

1. "FACT SHEET: The U.S. Department of Education Announces Partnerships Across States, School Districts, and Colleges of Education to Meet Secretary Cardona's Call to Action to Address the Teacher Shortage," U.S. Department of Education, accessed August 13, 2022, https://www.ed.gov/coronavirus/factsheets/teacher-shortage.

CHAPTER 7

1. B. Kasanoff, "To Communicate More Effectively, Use the Theory of Seven," *Forbes*, June 26, 2014, https://www.forbes.com/sites/brucekasanoff/2014/06/26/the-theory-of-seven/?sh=4d21bddd6faf.

2. Ronald Heifetz and Marty Linsky, "A Survival Guide for Leaders," *Harvard Business Review*, June 2022.

CHAPTER 9

1. *Merriam-Webster Online Dictionary*, s.v. "crisis," accessed July 27, 2022, https://www.merriam-webster.com/dictionary/crisis.

2. J. Bernstein, "Creeping, Slow-Burn, and Sudden Crises," *Free Management Library Blog*, July 26, 2022, https://www.bernsteincrisismanagement.com/creeping-slow-burn-and-sudden-crises/; Erika Hayes James and Lynn Perry Wooten, "Leadership as (Un)usual: How to Display Competence in Times of Crisis," *Organizational Dynamics* 34, no. 2 (2007): 141–52.

About the Authors

Rich Drolet, EdD, has served as a superintendent of schools in Massachusetts since 2018. Prior to becoming superintendent, he was a district-wide curriculum director, principal, and assistant principal at the middle level, and teacher at the middle and elementary levels. Drolet earned his doctorate from Johnson

& Wales University. His dissertation, related to increasing the effectiveness of teacher common planning time, received the 2010 National Association of Secondary School Principals' Dr. Ted Sizer Middle Level Dissertation of the Year Award.

Drolet won the 2013 Rhode Island Middle School Principal of the Year Award, and he has taught education courses as an adjunct professor at the University of Rhode Island. He has given presentations on grading and middle-level reform; instructional leadership and educator evaluation; positive behavioral interventions and supports; the responsive classroom; professional learning communities; best practices for superintendent and school committee chair relations with municipal leaders; and racial equity, diversity, and inclusiveness. Drolet has served as a new teacher mentor, boot camp facilitator for at-risk students, and basketball coach. He can be reached at rkdrolet@yahoo.com.

Armand Pires, PhD, has served as a superintendent of schools in Massachusetts since 2015. Prior to this, he served as assistant superintendent, director of curriculum, principal, and assistant principal at the middle and high school levels, as well as a teacher at the middle and high school levels. Pires holds a PhD in education from the University of Rhode Island.

Pires's research interests include leadership development, student mental health, and professional development. He is active in the Massachusetts state superintendent professional organization and serves as an officer. He also supports the development of school leadership by mentoring principals in training. Pires is an avid cyclist and reader. He can be reached at armandrpires@gmail.com.

www.ingramcontent.com/pod-product-compliance
Lightning Source LLC
Chambersburg PA
CBHW020749230426
43665CB00009B/540